Data Modelling

London: The Stationery Office

CCTA
Central Computer and Telecommunications Agency

First published 2000

ISBN 0 11 330871 X

Titles within the Business Systems Development series include:

SSADM Foundation	ISBN 0 11 330870 1
Data Modelling	ISBN 0 11 330871 X
The Business Context	ISBN 0 11 330872 8
User Centred Design	ISBN 0 11 330873 6
Behaviour and Process Modelling	ISBN 0 11 330874 4
Function Modelling	ISBN 0 11 330875 2
Database and Physical Process Design	ISBN 0 11 330876 0
Also available as a boxed set	ISBN 0 11 330883 3

For further information on CCTA products
Contact:

CCTA Help Desk
Rosebery Court
St Andrews Business Park
Norwich NR7 0HS
Tel 01603 704567 GTN 3040 4567

CONTENTS

FORWARD

The Business Systems Development (BSD) series represents 'best practice' approaches to investigating, modelling and specifying Information Systems. The techniques described within this series have been used on systems development projects for a number of years and a substantial amount of experience has contributed to the development of this guidance.

Within the BSD series the techniques are organised into groups that cover specific areas of the development process, for example *User Centred Design* which covers all aspects of the investigation, specification and design of the user interface.

The techniques provide a practical approach to the analysis and design of IT systems. They can also be used in conjunction with other complementary techniques such as Object-Oriented techniques.

The material used within this series originated in the Structured Systems Analysis and Design Method (SSADM) which was introduced by the CCTA as a standard method for the development of medium to large IT systems. Since its introduction in the early 1980's, SSADM has been developed through a number of versions to keep pace with the evolving technology and approaches in the IT industry.

The *SSADM Foundation* volume within the BSD series describes the basic concepts of the method and the way in which it can be employed on projects. It also describes how the different techniques can be used in combination. Each of the other volumes in the series describes techniques and approaches for developing elements of the overall specification and design. These can be used in conjunction with one another or as part of alternative approaches. Cross-referencing is provided in outline within the description of each of the techniques to give pointers to the other approaches and techniques that should be considered for use in combination with the one being described.

All volumes within the Business System Development series are available from:

The Stationery Office
St Crispins
Duke Street
Norwich
NR3 1PD

Acknowledgments

Laurence Slater of Slater Consulting Ltd is acknowledged for editing existing material and where necessary developing new material for the volumes within the Business Systems Development series. John Hall, Jennifer Stapleton, Caroline Slater and Ian Clowes are acknowledged for much of the original material on which this series is based.

The following are thanked for their contribution and co-operation in the development of this series:

Paul Turner	-	Parity Training
Tony Jenkins	-	Parity Training
Caroline Slater	-	Slater Consulting Ltd

In addition to those named above a number of people agreed to review aspects of the series and they are thanked accordingly.

1   INTRODUCTION AND OVERALL CONCEPTS

This volume is concerned with the modelling of data within the context of a IT development project. The modelling of data is at the very heart of any project and does exactly as its name implies – it models data without concern for the processing that must be applied to maintain the data.

Two specific areas of data modelling are covered:

- Production of the Logical Data Model

- Relational Data Analysis

This volume looks at the logical modelling of data and not the way in which the data will be physically implemented[1].

The main Logical Data Model which is developed on nearly every project is the *Required System Logical Data Model* which shows the way the data is organised for the new system taking into account any current system and all new requirements. On an application development project this is the main data model to be developed. Relational Data Analysis can be used to validate it. This is the data model which will go forward to Database Design and which will be maintained throughout the lifetime of the system.

A second Logical Data Model can be produced on a project. This is the *Current Environment Logical Data Model* which shows the way data is organised in any current system (automated or manual). This can then be added to any new requirements and these two used as the basis to draw up the Required System Logical Data Model. As before, if desired, Relational Data Analysis can be used to validate (or even be the basis of) the Current Environment Logical Data Model.

In this series all products are shown in the context of the System Development Template (SDT). This is a template which divides the system development process into activity areas onto which the development products may be mapped. Annexe A provides a fuller description of the System Development Template. Figure 1-1 shows how the Logical Data Model and Relational Data Analysis fit into the System Development Template.

All the examples within this volume are described in terms of EU-Rent which is a case study based around a car-rental business. For a full description EU-Rent see Annexe B.

---

[1] For a description of how the data model will be physically implemented see the *Database and Physical Process* Design volume in this series.

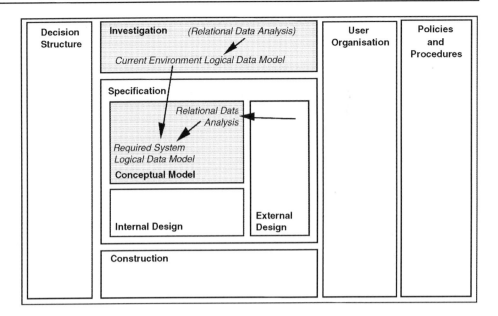

Figure 1-1 Place of the Logical Data Model and Relational Data Analysis in the System Development Template

As the diagram suggests, Relational Data Analysis is considered a supplementary technique to Logical Data Modelling. The results of Relational Data Analysis are used to enhance the Logical Data Model.

Organisation of this volume

After this (introductory) chapter the following is the organisation for this volume.

Chapter 2 – Logical Data Modelling. This is a full description of the concepts, products and techniques necessary to produce the Required System Logical Data Model and the Current Environment Logical Data Model.

Chapter 3 – Relational Data Analysis. This is a full description of the concepts, products and techniques of Relational Data Analysis and the steps necessary to enable it to validate the Logical Data Model.

Chapter 4 – Further Data Modelling Considerations. This chapter contains extra (more advanced) detail about different areas of Data Modelling that may prove useful to people constructing data models.

Chapter 5 – Meta Model. To assist projects and CASE tool developers, a meta-model is provided which shows the basic concepts covered in this volume and way they inter-relate.

Chapter 6 – Product Descriptions. Product descriptions are provided for all the major products described in this volume. These should be used by projects as a basis for the product descriptions to be used on the project. (Note: It is expected that the project will need to tailor these product descriptions so that items not required are omitted and any other items required by the project included.)

Annexes. There are three annexes appended to this volume. The first gives a description of the System Development Template, the second is a description of EU-Rent which is the case study that is used throughout this volume. The third is a glossary of terms that are relevant to this volume.

2   LOGICAL DATA MODELLING

Logical Data Modelling is used to investigate and model the way in which the data is defined, held and structured within a system.

The technique of Logical Data Modelling is firstly used to model the data/information of the current system (manual or automated) and then to build a model of what is required by the new system.

Logical Data Modelling is fundamental to nearly every Information System/Information Technology project. A Logical Data Model will be created on just about every project firstly to show an understanding of the data requirements for the system and then to be used as the basis for Database Design.

The Logical Data Model:

- being mainly diagrammatic, provides a clear, precise and simple representation which serves as a good communication vehicle and means of agreement with users;

- serves as a basis for database design but is independent of any specific implementation technique or product;

- acts as a definition of relevant terminology for use in user guides.

Logical Data Modelling:

- helps the analyst understand an application area by formalising his or her thinking;

- by achieving a common understanding between development staff early in the project reduces later problems.

This chapter focuses on the application of Logical Data Modelling for the definition of the data/information requirements for a computer system. However this technique can be used to support other projects including the development of strategic studies and the modelling of information requirements for non-database or non-computer systems. A further usage of the technique is in the production meta-models which show how concepts relate to each other. (See Chapter 5 for an example.) Corporate Data Modelling also uses the principles of Logical Data Modelling

2.1   Concepts for Logical Data Modelling

In this chapter, the products of Logical Data Modelling are described. In order to construct these products, however, it is important to understand some of the underlying concepts of Logical Data Modelling.

The following paragraphs explain some of these important concepts..

2.1.1 Entity

An entity is an object or concept, either concrete or abstract, which is of importance to the area of business being investigated. Each entity has a name, which should be singular. Each occurrence of an entity must be capable of being uniquely identified. Examples from EU-Rent include Car and Car Model.

2.1.2 Relationship

A relationship is a direct association between two entities, or between an entity and itself, to which all occurrences of the entities must conform. An occurrence of a relationship is an association between entity occurrences. An example for EU-Rent is that Car Model can have a number of Cars associated with it, whilst any one Car can only belong to one Car Model.

Each relationship will be between two entities. Generally for a relationship it will connect from one entity occurrence to many of the related entity occurrences (see later for further explnation). The entity at the 'one' end is known as the *master* entity and the entity at the many end is known as the *detail* or *child* entity.

2.1.3 Attribute

An attribute is a characteristic of an entity, that is any detail that serves to describe, qualify, identify, classify, quantify or express the state of an entity. Each attribute is a characteristic of one and only one entity unless it has different roles within that entity, or appears as part of the key structure or as a foreign key for that entity. Thus, attributes can appear in more than one entity only if they are part of a compound key or foreign key or assume several different roles within the same entity.

All attributes will be described as data items in the Data Catalogue and may be subject to definitions in the Domain Descriptions (see later).

An attribute can be mandatory or optional within each entity:

- it is mandatory if a value must be present for each occurrence of the entity;
- it is optional if it can remain or become 'blank' at any time during the entity's life.

Attributes can be mutually exclusive. For example, the entity 'rental' will be related to either a 'car group' or a 'car model' entity, but not both..

2.1.4 Keys

An entity occurrence is unique. Not only is an entity something which is essentially different in nature from other entities but an entity occurrence is something which can be distinguished from other entity occurrences of the same type. There must therefore be at least one unique identifier for each entity. The unique identifier may be:

- one or more mandatory attributes belonging to the entity;

- a combination of one or more mandatory attributes belonging to the entity and attributes representing the entity's participation in one or more mandatory, non-transferable relationships;

- attributes representing the entity's participation in two or more mandatory, non-transferable relationships.

One of the unique identifiers for each entity is nominated as the primary key. The primary key is one or more attributes within an entity. Each value of the primary key identifies a single occurrence of the entity.

Each entity may also contain one or more foreign keys. A foreign key is a set of one or more attributes which are a copy of the primary key of a master entity. The inclusion of a foreign key represents the relationship from the entity to its master. Foreign keys can only be attributes in an entity which are not part of the primary key. Primary keys can also contain attributes which form the keys of other entities, also representing relationships.

2.1.5 Entity Sub-Types

Sub-types and super-types are identified either by several different entities being found to have common identifiers (where identifiers have not been artificially generated) or a single entity having several different and distinct behaviours which are alternatives for one another (often indicated by each sub-type having different attributes and relationships).

In both cases, a super-type is identified which is a general description of all sub-types. The super-type contains the primary key of the entity (see above for description of keys) and any attributes which are common to all sub-types.

Within EU-Rent a Car Booking can be of three different types; a rental, a transfer to another branch or for a service. Each of these three are regarded as sub-types of the super-type Car Booking.

It should be noted that a super-type does not have an independent existence from its sub-types. It is not possible to have an occurrence of the super-type – all entity occurrences will be one or other of the sub-types together with the super-type.

2.1.6 Entity Aspects

Some real-world entities need to be modelled in more than one sub-system. The term 'aspect' is used for the representation of the entity in a single sub-system.

The concept of aspect incorporates the behaviour to be modelled as well as the pure 'data' view. Aspects identify different behaviours of the same real world entity. For example, an employee can work on projects and participate in a training scheme. These are not alternative behaviours, but they are different, parallel, co-existing behaviours of the same entity.

Aspects in different sub-systems usually need to be co-ordinated. There are often shared characteristics, for example employee name, which are common to all aspects. Also what happens in one application may constrain what can be done in another, for example when defining an employee's assignments, the project control application may need to check the training application for courses that the employee has been booked onto.

Even where there is only a single un-partitioned system, entity aspects can be a useful concept in developing a Logical Data Model. In fact, all entities on a Logical Data Model can be considered to be entity aspects as they represent only the view taken of that entity from the system under investigation. Generally in one Logical Data Model we only need to model one view of each real-world entity so no confusion is caused by giving the entity box the name of the real-world entity and referring to 'entities' rather than 'entity aspects'.

2.1.7 Domain

Informally, a domain represents a 'pool of values' from which the actual values for attributes are drawn. A domain represents the validation and formatting rules, permitted classes and ranges of values (e.g. Mon.– Fri.) that are common to more than one attribute.

Domains may be useful in the identification of redundant attributes. If two different attributes are based on the same domain, then there may in fact be only one real attribute, and therefore one of the two is redundant. Domains can be hierarchical in that domains at one level can be generalised further at a higher level.

2.1.8 Transferable and non-transferable relationships

Where a relationship from detail to master can be transferred from one occurrence of the master entity to another occurrence of the same entity, the relationship to the master is considered to be transferable. If this is not allowed, then it is non-transferable. For example, if a Car entity is a detail of Car Model and Branch entities:

- the relationship between Car and Car Model is non-transferable as the car will not be able to change its model;

- the relationship between Car and Branch is transferable because the Car is able to transfer from one branch to another.

2.2   Products for Logical Data Modelling

The main product of Logical Data Modelling is the Logical Data Model. This comprises three parts:

- Logical Data Structure (LDS);

- Entity Descriptions;

- Relationship Descriptions.

This is represented diagrammatically in Figure 2-1.

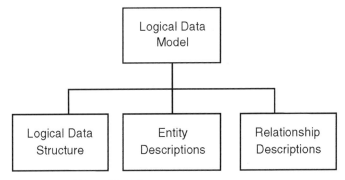

Figure 2-1 Logical Data Model

Two different Logical Data Models may be produced:

- **Current Environment Logical Data Model**: to provide a description of the information used or produced by the current environment.

- **Required System Logical Data Model**: to provide a detailed description of the information requirements of the new system. This tends to be more detailed than the Current Environment Logical Data Model. If any form of data modelling is used on a project then the Required System Logical Data Model should be regarded as a mandatory product.

In addition an Overview Logical Data Model can be produced during Project Initiation or Feasibility Study to give a quick appreciation of the data requirements for the new system. This can then be used for assisting with, for example, project resource estimating.

One further product that can be produced during Logical Data Modelling is the Data Catalogue. The Data Catalogue describes all the data items used and is maintained throughout the whole project with items being added and taken away as appropriate.

The Data Catalogue comprises two parts:

- Attribute/Data Item Descriptions
- Domain Descriptions

These are represented diagrammatically in Figure 2-2.

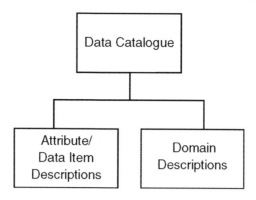

Figure 2-2 Data Catalogue

Logical Data Modelling represents types of entity, relationship and attribute, not individual occurrences. For example entity type names of 'Order' and 'Customer' are used, rather than the specific occurrences of 'Order Number 3412' and 'John Smith' as customer. The entity, relationship and attribute types are used to explain the meaning of data groups in the current environment and required system.

This publication will use the terms entity, relationship and attribute to mean entity, relationship and attribute types. Wherever specific occurrences of these are described, the terms 'entity occurrence', 'relationship occurrence' and 'attribute occurrence' will be used.

The following paragraphs describe each of the individual parts of the Logical Data Model and Data Catalogue.

2.2.1 Logical Data Structure

The Logical Data Structure formalises the structure of information by depicting diagrammatically the different types of relationship in which entities can participate.

A Logical Data Structure consists of two basic components:

- entities;
- relationships.

The basic notation is shown in Figure 2-3.

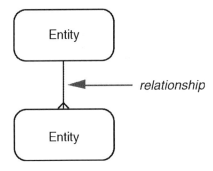

Figure 2-3 Basic components of a Logical Data Structure

Entities

An entity is represented diagrammatically by a soft box containing the name of the entity.

Two further concepts in the area of entities are:

- Entity Aspects;

- Entity Sub-types.

- These are illustrated in Figure 2-4 below and explained in the following paragraphs.

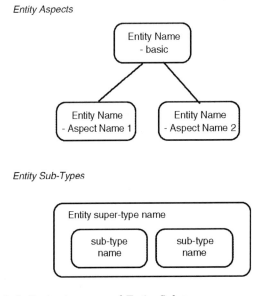

Figure 2-4   Entity Aspects and Entity Sub-types

Entity Aspects

An entity can have several different aspects. An aspect is a 'view' of an entity which can be one of the following:

- the behaviour of a real-world entity within a sub-system which needs to be co-ordinated with other views of the same entity in other sub-systems;

- the behaviour of one view of an entity in a single system which has several parallel and unconnected lives.

An example of entity aspects from the EU-Rent system is as follows. There are three different behaviours of the entity Service Depot which are:

- as a geographical location with an address;

- as a car maintenance provider with defined capacity (equipment and manpower), to which car service and repair work is allocated;

- as premises that need to be maintained, furnished and decorated and on which rent and property taxes need to be paid.

It has been decided that maintenance scheduling and property management are to be developed as two separate sub-systems which will need to be co-ordinated on implementation. The entity Service Depot will need to be separated out into different aspects, one 'basic' aspect which represents the common areas between the two areas and one aspect for each sub-system. The way that this is modelled on the Logical Data Structure covering both sub-systems is shown in Figure 2-5.

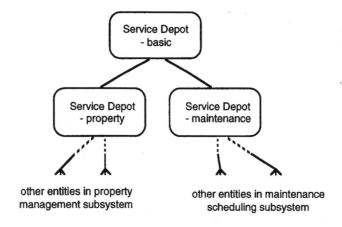

Figure 2-5 Example of Entity Aspects

In practice, two different Logical Data Models may be developed, one for each subsystem, each showing the entity Service Depot. A centralised Logical Data Model will show these as aspects and co-ordinate the definitions in each Logical Data Model.

On a Logical Data Structure, aspects are denoted by a dash'-' after the entity name, followed by the aspect name. Different aspects of the same entity can be shown connected by a mandatory one-to-one relationship to the 'basic' aspect which represents the common areas between all aspects. For clarity, it may be useful to label the relationship to emphasise that this represents a relationship between two aspects.

Entity sub-types and super-types

An entity may be found to have several different alternative behaviours such that each occurrence of the entity is of one particular type. The entity can be represented as a super-type and the alternative behaviours represented as sub-types.

Super-types are represented by a large soft box on the Logical Data Structure within which the sub-types are represented by smaller boxes. Sub-types can be nested in that sub-types can be sub-typed further if required.

An example of a simple super-type and corresponding sub-types from the EU-Rent system is shown in Figure 2-6 in which a Rental is either a Walk-in Rental or an Advance Booking Rental.

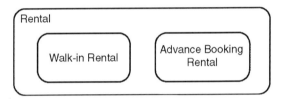

Figure 2-6 Example of super-type and sub-types

On the Logical Data Structure, any relationships which are the same for all sub-types are connected to the super-type (the outer box) and any for only one sub-type to that particular sub-type box. Logically, the super-type does not exist in its own right – there will never be an occurrence of the super-type which is not one of the sub-types.

Each sub-type contains any attributes which are specific to that sub-type only. Any relationships which are only true for that sub-type are connected to that sub-type on the Logical Data Structure. Sub-types are always alternatives for one another. This means that each value of the key of the super-type entity identifies only one of the sub-types. It is not possible for two different sub-type entity occurrences to co-exist.

There are no strict conventions for naming super-types and sub-types. However, it is helpful if names are chosen where the concatenation of the sub-type and super-type names gives a meaningful name. In the example above, the super-type is Rental and the sub-types are Walk-in and Advance Booking. The concatenation of the names gives the sub-types as Walk-in Rental and Advance Booking Rental – these names have been shown in full on the diagram for clarity but if the names become too long, the super-type name can be omitted from the sub-types.

Relationship

A relationship is represented diagrammatically by a line that joins two entity boxes together or joins an entity box to itself. Relationships convey a significant amount of information about the nature of the association between two entities.

The interaction between entities and relationships is very important to the production of the Logical Data Structure. A number of conventions are fundamentally important to this interaction. These are:

- Cardinality;

- Optionality;

- Relationship Labels;

- Multiple Relationships;

- Exclusive Relationship Groups;

- Recursive Relationships.

These are explained in detail below.

Cardinality

Relationship ends are either one (plain line) or many (indicated by a crow's foot).

These conventions are used in combination to give the following types of relationship:

- one-to-many (1:m) in which one occurrence of an entity is associated with one or more occurrences of another entity;

- one-to-one (1:1) in which one occurrence of an entity is associated with one and only one occurrence of another entity;

- Many-to-many (m:n) in which one or more occurrences of an entity are associated with one or more occurrences of another entity.

These are shown in Figure 2-7.

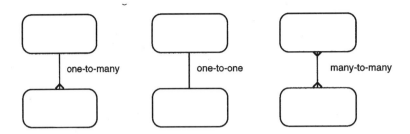

Figure 2-7: Cardinality of Relationships

In general, the Current Environment Logical Data Structure is likely to contain all three types of relationship shown in Figure 2-7. However, the Required System Logical Data Structure will only contain one-to-many relationships and minimal one-to-one relationships.

Optionality

Each relationship has two halves relating to the entities at each end of the relationship.

One half of a relationship is referred to as being mandatory if the connected entity's participation in the relationship is mandatory: an entity occurrence cannot exist without being a member of the relationship. A solid line is used to represent the mandatory half of a relationship: it shows that an entity occurrence at that end of the relationship must always be associated with an entity occurrence at the other end.

Similarly, one half of a relationship is referred to as being optional if the connected entity's participation in the relationship is optional: an entity occurrence can exist without being a member of the relationship. A dashed line is used to represent the optional half of the relationship: it shows on the diagram that entity occurrences at that end of the relationship need not be associated with entity occurrences at the other end.

Relationship ends are either mandatory or optional meaning that each relationship can be one of the following:

- fully optional (both entities can exist without each other);

- fully mandatory (both entities must exist at the same time);

- half mandatory – half optional.

All these possibilities are shown in Figure 2-8.

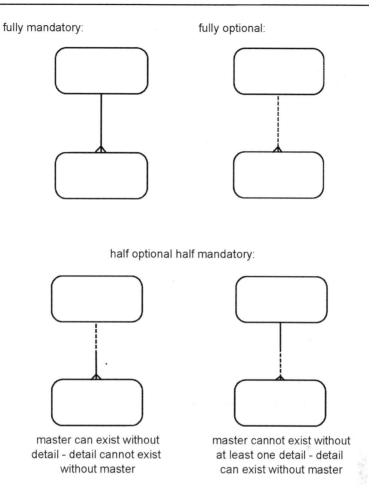

fully mandatory: fully optional:

half optional half mandatory:

master can exist without   master cannot exist without
detail - detail cannot exist   at least one detail - detail
without master   can exist without master

Figure 2-8 Optionality of Relationships

Master and Detail

It should be noted that a one-to-many relationship is between a 'master' entity and a 'detail' entity, the master being at the 'one' end and the detail being at the 'many' end. This is demonstrated in Figure 2-9.

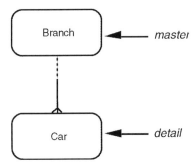

Figure 2-9 Master and Detail entities

Master and detail entities may be nominated for one-to-one relationships where required. The general convention is that the master is created first or is at the optional end of the one-to-one relationship.

Relationship labels

Each relationship has two labels, one at each end. Each label describes the relationship from the point of view of the entity it is nearest.

Each relationship label is chosen in order to give meaning and justification to the relationship. It is part of the definition of the entity at that end of the relationship.

Relationship labels should be phrased such that the statement reads correctly when preceded by the words 'must be' or 'may be'.

Relationship statements can be constructed mechanistically from the names of the entities at either end of the relationship, the cardinality and optionality of the relationship and the relationship labels. Each relationship has two relationship statements, one of which is read from the perspective of the first entity and the second which is read from the perspective of the second entity in the relationship.

If the 'subject entity' is taken to be the entity whose perspective is taken and the 'object entity' is taken to be the entity at the other end of the relationship, a relationship statement is constructed as follows:

- the word 'Each', followed by

- the name of the subject entity, followed by

- 'must be' if the relationship is mandatory from the end of the subject entity or 'may be' if the relationship is optional from the end of the subject entity followed by

- the relationship label from the end nearest the subject entity, followed by

- 'one and only one' if the relationship is 'one' at the other end of the relationship, or 'one or more' if the relationship is 'many' at the other end, followed by

- the name of the object entity.

The plural of the object entity name is used when reading a relationship where the degree is many.

The construction of relationship statements is demonstrated with reference to the relationship shown in Figure 2-10.

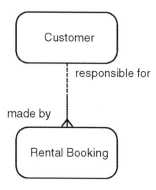

Figure 2-10 Demonstration of Relationship Statement construction

From this example, the following two relationship statements can be derived:

- Each Customer may be responsible for one or more Rental Bookings;
- Each Rental Booking must be made by one and only one Customer.

Note that the relationship optionality only applies within the scope of the system under investigation. For example, the relationship between Branch and Car entities in the EU-Rent system (see Figure 2-9) shows that the relationship is mandatory from the Car end, showing that all cars must be owned by a branch. This does not mean that every car known to EU-Rent must be owned by a branch; it means that the only cars within the scope of the investigation are owned by branches.

Multiple Relationships

The labelling of relationships is of particular importance where there are multiple relationships between two entities. The relationship labels are required to distinguish between the different relationships.

An example of multiple relationships is given in Figure 2-11.

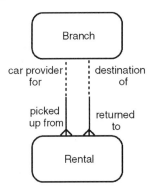

Figure 2-11 Multiple Relationships

In this example, each occurrence of the Rental entity must be associated with the branch from where the rental starts and is also connected to a branch for the return of the car (note: this can be different to the branch picked up from). The relationship statements for each of the relationships are as follows:

- For the first relationship describing where the rental starts:
    - Each Branch may be car provider for one or more Rentals.
    - Each Rental must be picked up from one and only one Branch.
- For the second relationship describing where the rental ends (if it is not at the first branch):
    - Each Branch may be destination of one or more Rentals.
    - Each Rental must be returned to one and only one Branch.

Exclusive relationship groups

If the participation of an entity occurrence in one relationship precludes its participation in one or more other relationships, this is known as an exclusive relationship.

An exclusive relationship group is represented on the Logical Data Structure by an exclusion arc. Exclusion arcs are drawn around an entity and apply to the relationship lines stemming from the entity which are crossed by the arc.

All relationships in an exclusive relationship group must have the same subject entity and same optionality.

Exclusive relationship groups are represented in Figure 2-12.

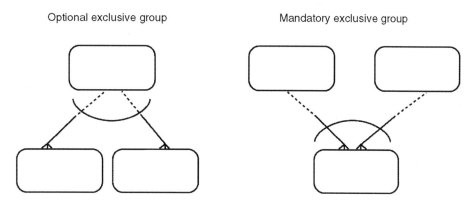

Figure 2-12 Exclusive relationship groups

Only one of the relationships in a group may exist at any one time for any occurrence of the common subject entity. In the case of mandatory exclusive groups, where the exclusion arc applies to several mandatory relationships, one of the relationships must apply.

An entity may participate in several different exclusive groups. The different exclusion arcs may, optionally, be labelled on the Logical Data Structure for reference purposes. In order to maintain the clarity of the Logical Data Structure, a relationship end should not participate in more than one exclusive group.

An example of an exclusive relationship group is shown in Figure 2-13.

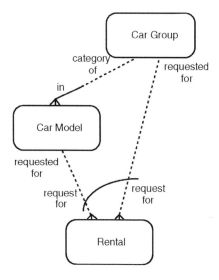

Figure 2-13 Example of exclusive relationships

In this example, the exclusive relationship shows that each occurrence of Rental may be either for a specific occurrence of Car Group or for an occurrence of Car Model.

Relationship statements for exclusive relationship groups should be dealt with in the following way:

- either concatenate the statements from the individual relationships, inserting 'or' between each individual statement, for example:

  - Rental may be request for one and only one Car Group, or Rental may be request for one and only one Car Model;

- or combine the statements into a single statement with the subject entity appearing only once and the remainder of the statement containing 'or' to show the exclusion, for example:

  - Rental may be request for one and only one Car Group or request for one and only one Car Model.

Recursive relationships

Recursive relationships are used where an entity is related to itself. An entity can be related to itself in two different ways:

- a hierarchy represented by a fully optional relationship starting and ending at the same entity (known as a 'pig's ear');

- a network represented initially by a many-to-many relationship starting and ending at the same entity. This is later resolved by adding a 'link' entity with two relationships to the first entity (known as a 'bill of material' or 'BOM' structure).

These are shown in Figure 2-14 and described in more detail in the following paragraphs.

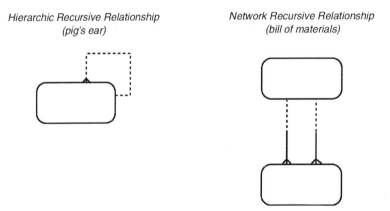

Hierarchic Recursive Relationship
(pig's ear)

Network Recursive Relationship
(bill of materials)

Figure 2-14 Recursive Relationships

A hierarchic recursive relationship represents a situation where occurrences of an entity can be related to other occurrences of the same entity in a one-to-many relationship. Each occurrence can only belong to one other occurrence of the entity. This type of structure can be used to represent the layers of management within an Organisation or geographical areas which break down into smaller areas and so on. The relationship is fully optional to allow for the fact that the occurrence at the top of the structure does not have a master and the occurrence at the bottom has no detail. An example from the EU-Rent system is shown in Figure 2-15.

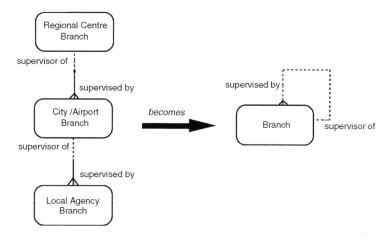

Figure 2-15 Example of hierarchic recursive relationship

The network recursive relationship represents the situation where occurrences of an entity can be related to other occurrences of the same entity in a many-to-many relationship. The many-to-many relationship is usually replaced with an entity which represents the relationship between the entity occurrences. This is most frequently encountered in the classic Bill of Materials Processing environment and is often called a 'bill-of-materials' structure. In the bill-of materials scenario, a variety of components/sub-assemblies are built into further sub-assemblies with the process continuing until the finished product is reached. Any sub-assembly may be a component part of many sub-assemblies whilst itself being made up of many other sub-assemblies.

An example of a network recursive relationship from the EU-Rent system is shown in Figure 2-16.

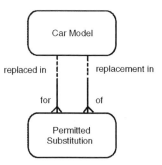

Figure 2-16 Example of network recursive relationship

This set of relationships allows a network of car models which may be considered substitutions for one another.

Note: in the examples given above, the Bill of Materials example has a 'top' and a 'bottom' - at the top will be a complete assembly, at the bottom individual nuts and bolts. In the example of the car models substituting for one another, there is no hierarchy – this is a more general example.

Example Logical Data Structure

An example Logical Data Structure from the EU-Rent case study is shown in Figure 2-17. This diagram demonstrates some of the notations described above.

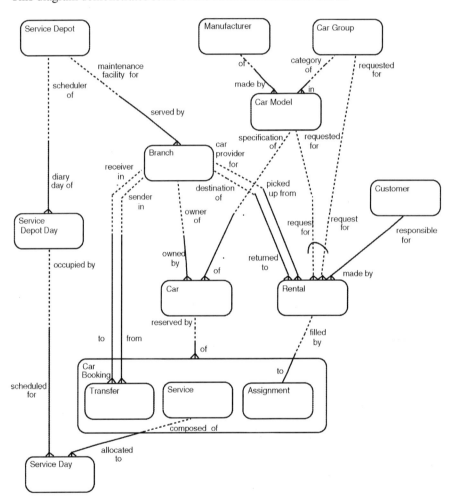

Figure 2-17 Logical Data Structure from the EU-Rent Case Study

2.2.2 Entity Descriptions

An Entity Description records information about the important characteristics of an entity on the Logical Data Structure. The Entity Description product is likely to be in the form of a report from a CASE tool, so it is not possible to be precise as to its format or even its precise content. The following list are those items that are generally recorded about an entity. With the exception of the Entity Name (and possibly the Description) they should all be regarded as optional. Projects may wish to record more or less detail as appropriate. Indeed it is expected that at the start of the project only a small amount of detail will be recorded with more being added as the project progresses.

Property	Description
Entity name	The unique and generally agreed name for the entity being described
Entity ID	A short reference name or number for the entity being described.
Aspects/sub-types/super-types	Where the entity has several aspects, each aspect should be described in a separate entity description and cross-referenced to the other aspects. Sub-types and super-types should each be described separately and cross-referenced to the other.
Average occurrences	An estimate of the average number of occurrences of the entity (for the system as a whole or for a particular location in a distributed application). Since 'average' is an imprecise concept, assumptions can also be recorded including relevant timeframe (e.g. six month moving average).
Maximum occurrences	An estimate of the maximum number of entity occurrences. Assumptions can be recorded such as the life of the system.
Description	A definitive statement of the significance of the entity in the form of one or two sentences describing why the entity was included in the model and helping the reader to visualise occurrences.
Synonym(s)	If applicable, all other names for the entity including abbreviations.

Property	Description
Attribute name(plus indication of Mandatory/Optional mutually exclusive and Primary/Foreign Key)	An attribute is a characteristic of an entity. All attributes will be described as data items in the Attribute/Data Item Descriptions (see later) If an attribute is known to be mandatory or optional within each entity occurrence, this should be indicated. An indication should be given where attributes are mutually exclusive. Each Attribute which forms part of the primary key and/or foreign keys should be annotated as such. Where access restrictions for specific attributes are known, details should be recorded
Relationship Statements	Relationship statements for which this entity is the subject can be listed as descriptions of the entity's associations with other entities.
User role	The user roles which will have access to occurrences of this entity. The access rights which the corresponding User Role in the row is to be granted can also be recorded. Access rights can be (I)nsert, (R)ead, (M)odify, (D)elete, (A)rchive, ALL.
Ownership	The person or user role responsible for the definition of the entity from within the business. Ownership of entity occurrences can also be recorded.
Growth per period	A description of growth rate(s) of entity occurrences and applicable period(s).
Archive and destruction	A statement of requirements in relation to archiving and destruction of entity occurrences.
Security measures	A statement of security requirements for this particular entity.
State indicator values	Valid state indicator values (or ranges) and their meanings.

Note: User role, access rights, owner, archive and destruction, and security measures need not be specified for individual entities.

Figure 2-18 shows an example of a completed Entity Description from the EU-Rent system.

Entity Name	**Rental**	
Entity ID	E017	
Average Occurrences	For current year:	
	Airport Branch (100): 67,500	6,750,000
	City Branch (200) 35,000	7,000,000
	Local Agency Branch (700) 8,250	5,775,000
	Current year total	19,525,000
	3 years' history	55,000,000
	Total	74,525,000
Maximum Occurrences	See growth below	
	Year 5	26,000,000
	3 years' history	68,000,000
	Total	94,000,000
Description	Rental of a car by a customer	
Synonym(s)	Car Rental, Walk-in Rental (for some occurrences)	
Super-type	None	
Sub-types	Free and paid: Free Rental, Paid Rental	
	Direction: Round-trip, One-way	

Attributes

Rental Number	system generated, unique
Driver ID	foreign key
Reservation Date	
Rental Basis	
Advance Request (mutually exclusive or both null)	
Car Group Number	foreign key
Car Model Number	foreign key
Rental Start Date	
Branch ID (pick-up)	foreign key
Rental End date	
One-way Rental (optional)	
Branch ID (return)	foreign key
Rental Outcome (mutually exclusive)	
Completed Rental	
Insurance Indicator	
Credit Card Reference	
Customer Address (local)	
Customer Telephone (local)	
Fuel	
Cancellation	
Cancellation Date	
Reason for Cancellation	

Relationship Statements	Each rental	
	must be made by a Customer	
	must be picked up from a Branch	
	must be returned to a Branch	
	may be a request for either a Car Group or a Model	
	may be filed by an Assignment Booking	
	may be extended by one or more Rental Extensions	
	may be the basis of one or more Additional Chanrges	
User role access	Branch Manager, Counter Clerk	Create, Modify, Read
	Benefit scheme administrator	Read
	Database administration	Archive, Delete
Ownership	Specification	Rental Operations Manager
	Ownership of individual occurrences	Pick-Up Branch
Growth per period	5% - 10% per year during 5-year life of system	
Archive and Destruction	Archived after three years	
	Deleted after 10 years	
Security Measures	User authorisation to access functions that use Rental	
State Indicator values	Reserved	
	Car allocated	
	In progress	
	History	

Figure 2-18 Completed Entity Description

2.2.3 Relationship Descriptions

The majority of information that is required about each relationship appears on the Logical Data Structure in the form of cardinality, optionality, exclusions etc. However, there may be a requirement to record more precise volumetric information about a relationship or access/security information about the relationship. In this case, a Relationship Description can be produced.

Again, there is no precise format required for a Relationship Description as it is likely to be a report from a CASE tool. Below is a list of the properties that you may wish to record about each relationship and an example of a Relationship Description taken from the EU-Rent case study.

(Note that each Relationship Description applies from one end of a relationship to the other. To gain a complete description for a relationship, two Relationship Descriptions will be required: one from each end.)

Property	Description
Entity names types/sub-types)	The name of the subject and object entities. This needs to be qualified by the relationship label in the case of multiple relationships in order to uniquely identify the relationship being described.
% optional	This box is completed if the relationship end is optional from the subject entity end and gives the percentage of entity occurrences of the subject entity not participating in the relationship. This means that if 90% of the occurrences of the subject entity are expected to participate in the relationship, the figure here would be 10%.
Description	This is only completed if the Relationship Statement requires further explanation.
Synonym(s).	A list of alternative phrases for the relationship of the Entity Description label if required
Minimum occurrences	The minimum number of entity occurrences at the object end of the relationship for each occurrence of the subject entity where the relationship is 'many' at the object end.

Property	Description
Average occurrences	An estimate of the average number of entity occurrences at the object end of the relationship for each occurrence of the subject entity. Often the mean will be acceptable. However, if the distribution of relationship occurrences is skewed, a different number may be more useful. For example, if there are 6 entity occurrences in 10% of relationships and 1 occurrence in 90% of relationships, the mean is 1.5, but it will be more useful to take the average as 1 (the mode) for working purposes.
Maximum occurrences	The maximum number of entity occurrences at the object end of the relationship for each occurrence of the subject entity.
Cardinality	More precise details of the distribution of relationship description occurrences if required (for critical relationships this might be a reference to a graphical analysis).
Growth per period	A description of the growth rate(s) of relationship occurrences and applicable period(s).
Additional properties	Additional properties of the relationship end e.g. whether transferable.
User role	The user roles which will have access to occurrences of the relationship end being described.
Owner	The person or user role responsible for deciding the types of access which will be permitted.

User role, access rights and owner are unlikely to be specified for most relationships. If they are specified, they are likely to be the same for both ends of the relationship.

Figure 2-19 gives an example of a completed Relationship Description taken from the EU-Rent system. The Relationship Description documents a single relationship but has two entries as the relationship is described from each end.

Entity names	Rental must be returned to one Branch
% optional	90% (only 10% of rentals are on-way)
Description	This relationship is created to show that a Rental can be returned to any Branch - either the one it was rented from or another Branch.
Synonym(s)	Dropped off at
Additional Properties	Changeable - a car could be dropped off at a one different to the one oroginally agreed

Entity names	Branch may be the destination of one or more Rentals
% optional	Expected to be 100% but a car can be written-off during the rental
Description	This relationship indicates the Branch to be dropped off at. The relationship is left open so that the destination Branch can be the same as the one the car was picked up from or a different one if required
Synonym(s)	Drop-off branch for, One-way destination of
Mimimum Occurrences	0
Average Occurrences	2,000
Maximum Occurrences	6,000
Cardinality Description	Airports and seaports tend to have twice as many as other branches
Growth per period	5% - 10% over a five year period
Additional Properties	If a customer booked a car to be dropped off at one Branch but then returned it to another Branch there is no need to keep a record of the original drop-off Branch

Figure 2-19 Relationship Description

2.2.4 Attribute/Data Item Descriptions

All data items used within the system will be described in the Data Catalogue. A significant sub-set of the data items will be used as attributes of entities and referenced on Entity Descriptions.

The precise format of an Attribute Data Item Description will depend upon the tools available for its production. Below is a list of properties that you may wish to record about each data item followed by an example of an Attribute/Data Item Description taken from the EU-Rent case study.

Property	Description
Attribute/data item name	The unique and generally agreed name for the data item.
Attribute/data item ID.	A short reference name or number for the data item. This field is optional

Property	Description
Cross-references	This is used to cross-reference products which contain the data item e.g. Entity Description. A cross-reference to another Attribute/Data Item Description would be used if there is both a logical and physical designation. There may even be several different physical descriptions of the Data Item in the current environment.
Synonym(s)	A list of other names for the data item including abbreviations if required.
Description	Further information describing the data item if required.
Validation/ derivation	Validation should include permitted values, ranges, codes, sequence and consistency checks. Derivation rules will be described if the value of the attribute is calculated from the values of other attributes or generated by the system. Attributes which are derived once, when the entity is created, should be distinguished from attributes which are repeatedly recalculated. Some validation/derivation rules may be described in a common Domain Description.
Default Value	If necessary a 'Default Value' is specified. This is the value that the data item will take if left blank in any context. This is most likely to be used in Dialogue Design.
Logical format	A description of the logical format.
Logical length	The logical length in terms of number of characters.
Length description	Where the length may vary, a statement of the average and maximum length.
User role	The user roles which will have access to this data item.
Access rights	The access rights which the corresponding user role in the row is to be granted. Access rights can be (I)nsert, (R)ead, (M)odify, (D)elete, (A)rchive, ALL.
Owner.	The person or user role responsible for deciding the types of access which will be permitted

Property	Description
Standard messages	May be used to specify help, error, normal prompt and other messages that will be displayed to the user as part of an on- line dialogue involving this data item.

Figure 2-20 gives an example of an Attribute/Data Item Description taken from the EU-Rent system.

Attribute/Data Item Name	**Customer Address**	
Attribute/Data Item ID	045	
Cross-references	Entities	Customer, Rental (local address)
Description	Address of customer, excluding country and postcode	
Synonym(s)	Contact Address, Local Address	
Validation/Derivation	Must consist of only alpha and numeric characters with no punctuation and no control characters other than the returns between lines	
Default Value	For Input, the value stored in Customer or Rental, if one exists, otherwise spaces	
Logical Format	Character string	
Logical Length	Average of 50 characters	
Length description	Maximum 120 characters	
User role access	Branch Manager, Counter Clerks Benefits Programme administrator	Create, Modify, Read Modify, Read
Owner	Depends on context	
Standard Message	Validation: "Should contain only alpha and numeric characters"	

Figure 2-20 Example Attribute/Data Item Description

2.2.5 Domain Descriptions

The concept of a domain is used in Logical Data Modelling to represent validation and formatting rules, permitted classes and ranges of values (e.g. Mon.–Fri.), which are common to more than one attribute. These are defined in exactly the same way as individual data items and referenced by specific data items as a 'short hand' for whichever details are described in the domain.

A common example of a domain is 'date'. A common format for all dates used within the system can be defined. This is referenced by all data items which are dates. The format does not need to be defined for each data item as it is defined once as a domain.

Domains are extremely useful for imposing consistency across systems as all data items of a specific type can be made to conform to a single central definition.

Domains can be hierarchical to allow different characteristics of a domain to be described more generally at a higher level.

The format of a Domain Description will be exactly the same as the Attribute Data Item Description.

2.3   Techniques for Logical Data Modelling

In Logical Data Modelling, the analyst considers the entities (the objects and concepts of importance in the area of the business or system being modelled) and then analyses the relationships between them (usually based on relationships and rules in the business environment). As part of defining the entities, the analyst identifies the major attributes (descriptive properties) of those entities. The results are documented as a Logical Data Model (LDM).

The activities involved in developing a Current Environment Logical Data Model and Required System Logical Data Model are, to some extent, similar. Therefore, in this section, the general activities of Logical Data Modelling are described first and then the particular concerns to be addressed in developing the two different Logical Data Models are discussed later.

The activities of Logical Data Modelling are as follows:

- perform fact finding;
- identify entities;
- identify relationships;
- draw the Logical Data Structure;
- normalise the Logical Data Model;
- validate the Logical Data Model against functional requirements.

For the sake of presentational convenience, these tasks have been separately identified and are described below. In practice, tasks will be conducted in parallel or may even be indistinguishable. Tasks may also be carried out in a different sequence or may be omitted when Logical Data Modelling is carried out at a particular Step.

2.3.1 Fact Finding

There are various ways of identifying entities, relationships and attributes, including:

- analysing forms;
- analysing open interview notes and paper sources such as annual reports;
- observation;
- personal knowledge and judgement; structured interviews.

2.3.2 Identifying Entities

It can be difficult to identify entities because people talk in terms of examples and analogies. Synonyms (different words with the same meaning) and homonyms (same word with different meanings) may also cause difficulty. Care should be taken to distinguish the roles of things, particularly people and organisations, from the actual entities.

The analyst must identify the essential underlying entities, select a generic word for it that everyone is happy with, and then define it.

It may help to think in terms of notional keys, the things in the environment which need to be individually identified. When the analyst discovers a 'name' or 'key' in analysing a system it is a thing which the user wishes to distinguish from other things of the same type, i.e. an entity. These keys should identify a group of data items needed by the system and thus an entity.

When a potential entity has been discovered, the answer **yes** to the following questions is a useful guideline to its validity:

- Does the business need to hold data about it?;

- Is it relevant to the business?;

- Is there more than one occurrence?

Where data modelling has previously been undertaken within the Organisation, entities may be identified from existing repositories and dictionaries. For organisations that have formal Data Management in place, the Corporate Data Model will be a source of entities and will constrain the identification of entities and attributes throughout the project.

2.3.3 Identifying Relationships

For each pair of entities (or an entity and itself), it is necessary to check whether it is possible for one entity to be related to another without the relationship being described in terms of some other entity (i.e. the relationship is direct).

A useful aid in identifying relationships between entities is a matrix which lists entities along both axes. Each intersection should be considered in turn to identify direct relationships between entities. A mark can be placed at the intersections that represent a relationship.

It is also necessary to consider:

- exclusive groups

- degree

- link phrases

- multiple relationships

- optionality.

Most of these will become apparent as the Logical Data Structure is drawn.

2.3.4 Drawing the Logical Data Structure

Many 'rough' models are drawn early on, especially in initial discussions with users which can be used as the basis for the Logical Data Structure. If a matrix has been used to identify relationships, this can also be a useful starting point for drawing a Logical Data Structure.

The following points should be borne in mind:

- aim for clarity, consistency and simplicity;

- it is recommended that all the relationship ends are named on the Logical Data Structure although this is not as important for relationships whose meanings are obvious;

- in general, masters should be above details so that the crow's feet are pointing downwards (this is only a general guideline and should not be followed at the expense of clarity);

- minimise crossing lines;

- neatness and layout are important;

- do not use abbreviations.

2.3.5 Naming Relationships

Naming relationships at both ends helps eliminate unnecessary relationships very early on, identifies weak understanding and frequently exposes the fact that further relationships and entities are needed. It is therefore important that relationship labels are properly defined.

Where a CASE tool is being used, it is optional as to whether all relationship labels are displayed on the Logical Data Structure provided the significance of the relationships is clear and their meaning recorded within the repository of the CASE tool.

2.3.6 Normalising the Logical Data Model

The final Required System Logical Data Model should be a normalised model which means that attributes should belong to only one entity (excluding keys and different roles of the same attribute) and relationships should all be one-to-many or one-to-one. The technique of Relational Data Analysis is used as a supporting technique to Logical Data Modelling and can be used to help ensure that the Logical Data Model is in a normalised form.

Relational Data Analysis is described in more detail in the Relational Data Analysis chapter.

2.3.7 Partitioning the Logical Data Structure

User and analyst understanding of a large Logical Data Structure can be improved by partitioning, creating sub-diagrams which show only a portion of the main diagram. One way of making this apparent is to use a notation for an 'incomplete' entity representing an entity that has relationships and connected entities not shown on the sub-diagram.

Incomplete entities are shown as dotted boxes. Only relationships for which both participating entities are on the diagram, are shown.

An example of a partitioned Logical Data Structure from EU-Rent is shown in Figure 2-21. In this example, the entities Service Depot and Service have relationships with other entities not shown on this diagram.

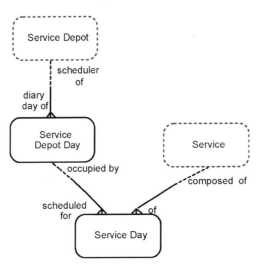

Figure 2-21: Example of partitioned LDS from EU-Rent

An alternative way of partitioning a Logical Data Structure is to use the concept of entity aspects. Instead of denoting an entity as partial, it is possible to separate out the different aspects of an entity that will appear on the different sub-models and to show the entity aspect name on each sub-model. In this case, it is not necessary to use the notation for partial entities. This is not generally used simply for presentational purposes but is the recommended approach for partitioning a Logical Data Structure into sub-systems which will be treated as distinct in subsequent development. An example of this from the EU-Rent system is shown in Figure 2-22.

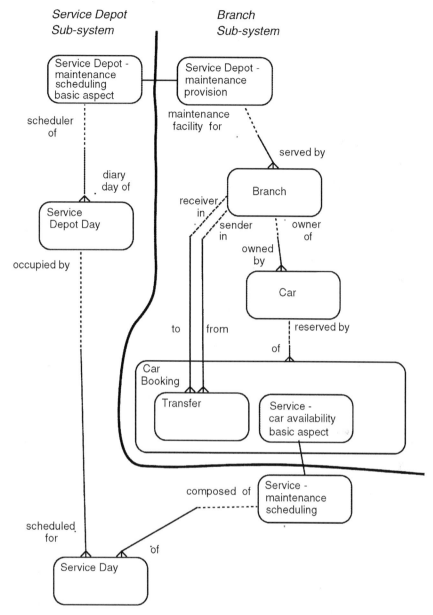

Figure 2-22 Example of partitioning using entity aspects

Note that, in this example, entity aspects are denoted using a one-to-one relationship directly between them instead of showing each entity aspect related through a separate 'basic' entity aspect. This convention is an acceptable alternative to the convention described in this chapter provided that one or other of the aspects is nominated as the basic aspect. Please see 4.1.1, for further explanation of this convention.

2.3.8 Validating the Logical Data Model against other project models

This is a very important part of developing a Logical Data Model and is vital in ensuring that the Logical Data Model is correct and will support the users' requirements for the new system. If any of the requirements cannot be satisfied by the Logical Data Model, then the model will need to be amended or the requirement dropped.

The sections below refer to models not covered in this volume but which are expected to be produced as part of the development project and which are covered in other volumes in the *Business System Development* series.

Validation against Data Flow Model (see the *Function Modelling* volume)

Each entity on the Required System Logical Data Model should be contained within one main data store in the Required System Data Flow Model.

The Logical Data Model can be validated against the Data Flow Model by checking the data items flowing into and out of the processes that access main data stores. The data items that are reflected on data flows are likely to indicate a need for that data to be stored within entities shown on the Logical Data Model.

Validation against Business Activity Model (see *The Business Context* volume)

The Business Activity Model should be a central source of requirements for a new automated information system. Requirements for enquiries are derived by identifying the information support needed by the business activities.

To develop a specification of the requirements for a new automated system, it is necessary to separate out categories of information which are to be provided by the new system from those which will be provided from elsewhere. The remaining requirements for information support will determine the content of the Logical Data Model.

Validation against Requirements Catalogue (see *The Business Context* volume)

Users often express requirements which involve data. Any requirement which specifies data that is required by the users should be checked to ensure the Logical Data Model is capable of delivering that data.

Validation against enquiries (see the *Behaviour and Conceptual Process Modelling* volume)

Each requirement for an enquiry should be used to check that the Logical Data Model is able to provide the data to satisfy that enquiry. Enquiries are a powerful tool in the development and validation of the Logical Data Model. The validation of the Logical Data Model against enquiries can be used to develop Enquiry Access Paths (see Behaviour and Process Modelling in this series) if this is considered useful.

Validation against Entity Life Histories (see the *Behaviour and Conceptual Process Modelling* volume)

The detailed analysis performed in the development of Entity Life Histories is likely to improve the analyst's understanding of the entities in the system. Also, the identification of parallel patterns of behaviour may trigger the identification of entity aspects.

2.4 Relationship with other analysis and design techniques

Logical Data Modelling is so fundamental to the development of a new system that it has some links to most of the other techniques used in analysis and design. Below are some of the major links.

The techniques listed below are all covered within the publications that are part of this series.

2.4.1 Data Flow Modelling (covered in the Function Modelling volume)

Each main data store on a Logical or Required System Data Flow Diagram corresponds to a portion of a Logical Data Structure. Data flows going into a main data store represent updates to entities on the Logical Data Structure. The Logical/Required System Data Flow Models are checked to ensure that each entity is contained within one data store and that there are processes which maintain each entity. The Logical Data Structure is checked to ensure that there is an access path to the required data for each elementary process.

2.4.2 Requirements Definition (covered in The Business Context volume)

In Requirements Definition, the Requirements Catalogue is used to record the requirements of the new system. Relevant requirements (new data requirements, data access restrictions etc.) are added to the Required System Logical Data Model.

2.4.3 Business System Options (covered in the SSADM Foundation volume)

Logical Data Structures may be produced to help define the scope of Business System Options (BSOs).

2.4.4 Function Definition (covered in the Function Modelling and User Centred Design volumes)

Each update and enquiry function is related to one or more events and/or enquiries, each of which will require an access path through the Logical Data Structure to obtain data. For enquiries, the access path is documented as an Enquiry Access Path. For events, the access path is usually defined by an Effect Correspondence Diagram. Both Enquiry Access Paths and Effect Correspondence Diagrams are produced as part of Behaviour Modelling.

2.4.5 Behaviour Modelling (covered in the Behaviour and Process Modelling volume)

Each Entity Life History shows the valid sequence of events affecting a given entity on the Logical Data Structure. By validating the Required System Logical Data Model, Entity Behaviour Modelling reveals new entities and relationships to add to the Required System Logical Data Model. Enquiries are a powerful way of checking that the Logical Data Model can provide the required data in the correct format.

2.4.6 Relational Data Analysis (see Chapter 3)

Relational Data Analysis is a supporting technique to Logical Data Modelling and helps to identify and specify information requirements. A Logical Data Structure can be expressed as a collection of normalised relations and vice versa. Logical Data Modelling works top down, identifying the major entities first and then gradually adding more detail. Relational Data Analysis works from the bottom up, synthesising arbitrary data groups into larger data groups that correspond to the entities and relationships of a Logical Data Model. Relational Data Analysis provides a valuable cross-check on the validity of the Logical Data Model.

2.4.7 Conceptual Process Modelling (covered in the Behaviour and Process Modelling volume)

Enquiry Access Paths, Effect Correspondence Diagrams, Enquiry Process Models and Update Process Models are all models of the processes which act upon the data in the Required System Logical Data Model. These models contain operations which act upon the attributes of the Logical Data Model and rely on the navigation around the Logical Data Model.

2.4.8 Database Design (covered in the Database and Physical Process Design volume)

The components of the Logical Data Model are mapped to a corresponding physical representation (if possible on a one-to-one basis):

Logical components	Likely physical representation
entity type	record type, table, file
attribute	physical data item, column
relationship	foreign key, index, pointer char

3 RELATIONAL DATA ANALYSIS

Relational Data Analysis is a complement and a check to Logical Data Modelling. The Logical Data Modelling technique concentrates on identifying the information needed by business processes as a 'top-down' view. Relational Data Analysis uses definitions of data that is required by the user from the system to build a 'bottom-up' view of the data requirements.

The purpose of Relational Data Analysis (RDA) is to:

- capture the user's detailed knowledge of the meaning and significance of the data;
- validate the Logical Data Model by checking that all the required data is present and is structured correctly;
- ensure the data is logically easy to maintain and extend:
    - ensure all data inter-dependencies have been identified;
    - ensure all ambiguities have been resolved;
    - eliminate unnecessary duplication of data.
- form the data into optimum groups to provide a basis for sharing data between different areas of the application.

Relational Data Analysis helps to check that the Logical Data Model can actually be built and maintained and that all attributes are fully defined. This is done by:

- analysing the inputs and outputs and decomposing them into normalised relations;
- building sub-models from groups of relations, using the keys of the relations to define relationships between them;
- mapping the sub-models onto the Logical Data Model and resolving any differences.

When this has been completed, the project can be assured that every input item has a place in the Logical Data Model where it can be stored and every output item can be derived from the Logical Data Model.

The technique as described in this chapter is primarily used to enhance and validate the Required System Logical Data Model after it has been created and checked initially against the functional requirements. However, Relational Data Analysis can be extremely useful in the investigation of the current data for systems which already consist of a large amount of data that is capable of being structured.

The principles of Relational Data Analysis can be used informally to assist in the construction of the Logical Data Model as it is developed throughout the project.

Position in System Development Template

Relational Data Analysis is used to investigate and organise data that is held within a system as a check to the Logical Data Modelling activity.

Relational Data Analysis is used primarily in the Specification part of the System Development Template within the Conceptual Model although the technique can also be used to assist in Investigation. This is represented in Figure 3-1 below.

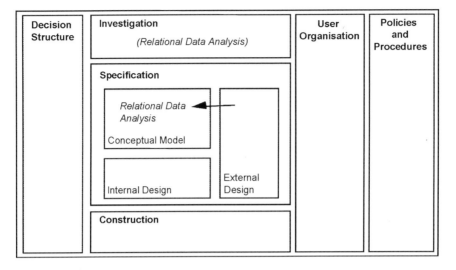

Figure 3-1 Relational Data Analysis in the System Development Template

As represented above Relational Data Analysis , which is in the Conceptual Model, receives most of its inputs from the products of External Design, e.g. User Object Models.

3.1   Concepts of Relational Data Analysis

Within Relational Data Analysis four concepts are very important:

- Normalisation;
- Relations;
- Primary and Candidate Keys;
- Foreign Keys.

These are explained in detail in the following paragraphs.

3.1.1 *Normalisation*

In Relational Data Analysis, normalisation is the process of producing the optimum grouping of attributes in relations. Normalisation has three main stages known as First, Second and Third Normal Form.[2]

Third Normal Form is reached by thoroughly analysing each item of data in order to:

- remove semantic ambiguities;

- identify inter-data dependencies;

- create a set of relations, each having a unique key and attributes which are totally dependent on the key.

The first stage in normalisation is to remove repeating groups of data items from the relation. Further normalisation addresses the functional dependencies between the attributes.

3.1.2 *Relations*

A relation is equivalent to an entity. It is defined as being a two dimensional table; that is, it comprises a number of rows and a number of columns. Each column represents an attribute of the relation and each row represents the values that can be taken by each attribute. An example of a relation from EU-Rent, the Car Relation is demonstrated in Figure 3-2.

---

[2] Those interested in the subject should refer to C. J. Date: *An Introduction to Database Systems*, volume 1; this provides a full explanation of the process of normalisation as well as a comprehensive, annotated, bibliography.

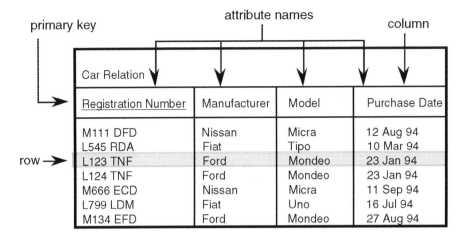

Figure 3-2 Example of a Relation

A table must have the following properties to be a relation:

- **no two rows are the same**. There must be no duplicate rows. A row is a duplicate of another if each of the attribute values in one row is identical to the corresponding attribute value in another row. Informally, each row in a normalised relation has a fixed number of attribute values and each of those values is a simple (non-compound) value. Where duplicate rows are found, they must either be merged or an extra column added to distinguish them;

- **the order of rows is not significant**. If rows have to occur in a certain order in the expectation that there is some significance in that order (age, seniority, cost etc.), then there is data missing from the relation It must be identified and added as an extra column;

- **the order of columns is not significant**. The same rule holds for the order of columns - if the order of columns has some significance the there is data missing from the relation. It must be identified and added as an extra column;

- **each column has a unique name**. The column names are used to identify data items and each column must therefore have a unique name. Where two columns are of the same domain e.g. account number, each must have a role name so that it may be uniquely named. For a direct debit mandate, the role names 'Transmitting' and 'Receiving' could be used, giving column names 'Transmitting-account-number' and 'Receiving- account-number'.

and to be a normalised relation (to First Normal Form), one additional property:

- **all attributes are atomic**. A relation may represent an arbitrary grouping of data (for example the data from a form or report). In such cases, one or more of its attributes may be broken down into other attributes. To what level attributes are broken down will depend upon the requirements of the system. For example, a UK car registration number contains a letter (the first letter) which may be used ti indicate the year of registration. The first letter of the registration number could, therefore, be treated as a separate attribute from the remainder of the registration number. However, within the EU-Rent system, a decision is made to treat the car registration number as an atomic item and not break it down any further.

A relation which contains a repeating group is referred to as an un-normalised relation.

In the example shown in Figure 3-3, for each value of the primary key, Model, there are potentially several values of Number of cars and Branches. The repeating elements are collectively termed a repeating group.

primary key   repeating group

Car Model Relation			
Model	Manufacturer	Number of cars	Branch
Micra	Nissan	7	Bristol
		4	London
Mondeo	Ford	11	Glasgow
		6	London
		14	Manchester
Uno	Fiat	9	Bristol
		12	Manchester

Figure 3-3 Example of Un-normalised Relation

It is desirable to have normalised relations. In a normalised relation all compound attributes are reduced to their basic component attributes. In the example in Figure 3-4, the number of cars has been separated out into number of cars at branch and number on order.

primary key

Stock Relation			
Branch	Model	Number at Branch	Number on Order
Bristol	Micra	7	0
London	Micra	4	2
Glasgow	Mondeo	11	0
London	Mondeo	6	8
Manchester	Mondeo	14	1
Bristol	Uno	9	2
Manchester	Uno	12	0

Figure 3-4 Example of Normalised Relation

In the example shown in Figure 3-4, a primary key is chosen for which there is only one value of each of the other attributes in the row. A combination of Branch and Model gives a single value for Number at Branch.

3.1.3 Primary and candidate keys

Every relation must have a primary key, a non-changeable attribute (or group of non-changeable attributes) whose values uniquely identify rows of the relation. For example, in the EU-Rent system, for the relation Car Manufacturer, Manufacturer Name is not a good choice for the primary key, since it may change from time to time. If the Manufacturer relation needs to mirror the real-world entity, even if it changes its name, we have to introduce Manufacturer ID to be the key.

Many relations have simple keys. A simple key is a single attribute. For example, the Manufacturer relation has Manufacturer ID as its primary key, Car has Registration Number as its primary key.

There may be more than one candidate key for a relation. A candidate key is any (minimal) set of one or more attributes that can for all time be used as such a unique identifier. 'Minimal' means that no sub-set of those attributes identified as a candidate key is also a candidate key.

For each relation, one candidate key must be selected as the primary key which is used consistently throughout the system. For example, rows of the Car relation could be uniquely identified by either Registration Number or by Body Number (stamped on, or attached to, the car body at the factory). Body Number is shown as part of the relation in Figure 3-6. In this situation EU-Rent has chosen Registration Number as the key as this is a more visible identifier and will be more acceptable to the users.[3]

In some cases, more than one attribute is required to uniquely identify a relation. There are two types of multi-part key: compound and hierarchical:

- in a **compound key**, each element is the key of another relation. Compound keys can be used to define many-to-many relationships. For example, the Stock relation represents the stock of a car model at a branch. Stock rows can be uniquely identified by the compound of Branch ID/Model ID;

- in a **hierarchical key**, one element (the qualifier) is the key of another relation, the other (the qualified part) provides unique identification of instances of a repeated group. Hierarchical keys define one-to-many relationships. For example, bookings are numbered serially for cars. The key of booking is the concatenation of Registration Number and Booking ID. Note that we could not use Registration Number and Booking Start Date – bookings can be rescheduled, so booking start date is changeable. The qualified part of a hierarchical key is meaningless by itself.

It should be noted compound keys and hierarchical keys can both have more than two attributes.

On models keys are normally identified by underlining the attributes within the relation.

---

[3] Note that Registration Numbers can be transferred when a vehicle is scrapped whereas the Body number cannot be transferred. This may influence the decision on which attribute is chosen as a key.

3.1.4 Foreign keys

A foreign key is defined as a non-key attribute (or group of related non-key attributes) in one relation which is the same as the key of another relation. This is demonstrated in Figure 3-5. Foreign Keys are normally identified by placing an asterisk before the attribute name.

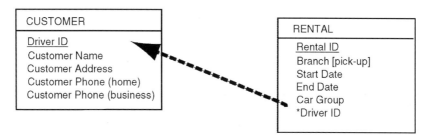

Figure 3-5 Example of Foreign Key

In this example, Driver ID is shown as a foreign key in Rental. This indicates that the Customer relation is related to Rental. The existence of the foreign key in Rental indicates that for each occurrence of Rental, there will be only one occurrence of Customer (the Rental must be for one and only one Customer). The fact that there is no corresponding foreign key in Customer indicates that for each occurrence of Customer, there may be many occurrences of Rental (a Customer is allowed any number of Rentals). The foreign key therefore indicates a one-to-many relationship between Customer and Rental.

A multi-part key (compound or hierarchical) may occur as a foreign key as shown in Figure 3-6.

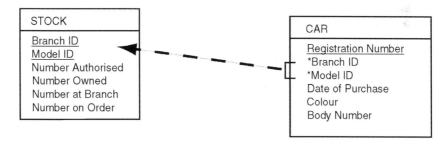

Figure 3-6 Example of multi-part Foreign Key

If there is a choice of candidate keys for a relation, we must be consistent in using the selected primary key as a foreign key in other relations. For example, if any other relation contains Body Number (a candidate key for car), it must be replaced by Registration Number (the candidate selected to be the primary key of car).

3.2   Products of Relational Data Analysis

The result of undertaking Relational Data Analysis is that the Required System Logical Data Structure is validated against the data flows into and out of the system and updated where necessary. As such there are no 'lasting' products from Relational Data Analysis – all products being regarded as transient.

The product that is used to help support the activities of Relational Data Analysis is the Relational Data Analysis Working Paper. The use of this product is demonstrated below (in the Relational Data Analysis Technique section) and a further example is shown at 3.4. The example of a Relational Data Analysis Working Paper included in this chapter was developed using a spreadsheet application. This can be used as a model for projects if required. However, it should be stressed that there is no standard format for a Relational Data Analysis Working Paper - Relational Data Analysis should be performed using whatever format is supported by the tools used to do the job. The items shown on the RDA Working Papers in this chapter are as follows:

- a column for each normal form (un-normalised, First Normal Form (1NF), Second Normal Form (2NF) and Third Normal Form (3NF));

- an indication of the level for each attribute in the un-normalised column – the level is determined by whether it is repeating or not and for repeating attributes, the level of nesting (this is explained further below);

- the results of the Relational Data Analysis exercise in terms of named relations.

The relations that are produced from Relational Data Analysis are converted to Logical Data Model (LDM) sub-models and compared with the Required System Logical Data Model as a process of validation and enhancement. These sub-models are produced in whatever format is helpful in the activity of checking against the Required System Logical Data Model. It would normally be expected that the LDM sub-models would be drawn to a simplified notation similar to the notation described for Logical Data Modelling. The LDM sub-models will be described in more detail as the technique is described below.

3.3   Relational Data Analysis Technique

Application of the Relational Data Analysis principles compels the analyst to consider:

- the means by which an occurrence of an entity is identified (entities, being objects or concepts of importance, must be identifiable). If the analyst cannot determine the attributes that identify an entity occurrence, he/she must consider whether the grouping of data does in fact represent an entity;

- whether the data in the data group belongs together – examining the dependencies that exist within data of a proposed entity type determines whether the data group represents a single entity or a number of different entities.

The steps involved in producing Third Normal Form relations are:

- select the sources for Relational Data Analysis and represent each of them as a set of un-normalised relations;

- convert to First Normal Form;

- convert to Second Normal Form;

- convert to Third Normal Form;

- rationalise results.

After these steps have been completed, it is necessary to be able to use the results of the Relational Data Analysis exercise to enhance the Required System Logical Data Model. The activities that can be used to achieve this are as follows:

- convert the Third Normal Form relations into partial Logical Data Models;

- compare the partial models with the Required System Logical Data Model and resolve differences.

All of these steps are described in the following paragraphs.

3.3.1 Notation and Conventions

For the purpose of the remainder of this chapter, the following conventions are used:

- relations are represented by a name given to the relation followed by a list of attribute names;

- a primary key is indicated by underlining its component attributes;

- a repeating group (or nested relation) is indicated by an indented set of attributes with its own primary key;

- hierarchical keys are bracketed;

- foreign keys are indicated by an asterisk.

These conventions are demonstrated in Figure 3-7.

Example of Relation:	Example of Repeating Group	Example of Foreign Key	Example of Hierarchical Key
primary key Manufacturer Manufacturer ID Manufacturer Name Manufacturer Address Contact Name Contact Phone Number	Branch Branch ID Branch Address Model ID Number Authorised Number Owned Number at Branch Number on Order	Rental Rental ID * Branch ID [pick-up] Start Date End Date * Customer ID * Car Group	Delivery (Branch ID) (Model ID) (Delivery ID) Purchase Ref Delivery Quantity Delivery Date

Figure 3-7 Conventions used to represent relations in this chapter

3.3.2 Select a source for Relational Data Analysis

The main source for Relational Data Analysis should be any document which shows the output requirements for the new system. This could include:

- Current reports required from the new system;

- Forms (e.g. invoices) required to produced by the new system;

- Output requirements for the new system.

If a Data Flow Model have been produced then the above can be derived from the I/O Descriptions which represent the flows into and out of the system. One problem that can occur from this approach is that if the analyst has made a mistake in constructing the Data Flow Model then this could be carried forward into the Relational Data Analysis. It is normally better to use the three items listed above backed up by the Data Flow Model.

Another source of output details is the User Object Model. Again there are problems in using this model in that it represents the users view of the data requirements and as such will tend to include non-persistent data such as calculated fields. In addition Relational Data Analysis requires data at an atomic level and users can describe data at a higher (compounded) level.

Whilst the major area of sources are the outputs, any input forms (and flows) should be considered when choosing the sources for Relational Data Analysis. One problem that does occur in using the input forms is that they may capture data which is not actually required for the system. If input forms are used then the data should be examined very critically to ensure that it is required.

In collecting together the forms, reports etc. that will make up the sources of Relational Data Analysis the analyst can end up with a great number of sources and using all of these can involve the project in using many man days effort on relational Data Analysis. In reality what is required is a good cross section of forms, report, data flows, etc. Criteria that may be used to sift possible sources are:

- Include important forms and reports (e.g. invoices)

- Include a few sources from each area of the business

- Check to see if the data from one source is basically the same as that from another source.

3.3.3 Represent source as un-normalised relations

Any data items which appear on the source are first listed in any order, although it is sometimes useful to list them in the order in which they occur on the source. Care should be taken to identify any implied (or hidden) data items, for example the position on a page, which are required in order to understand the data fully. The structure of the data items can be indicated in terms of a 'level'. A level indicates the structure of repeating groups within a set of data items/attributes. For each source, non-repeating data is level 1, repeating data is level 2 and onwards. Levels are illustrated with reference to a report of authorised car stocks at a branch taken from the EU-Rent system and illustrated in Figure 3-8.

Branch	O362	Hilltop Hotel Gloucester Place London NW1 6EP			
Model ID	Model Name	Manufacturer ID	Manufacturer Name	Group	Number Authorised
26	Escort	F01	Ford	B	12
39	Accord	H11	Honda	C	4
41	Uno	F02	Fiat	A	6
44	Scorpio	F01	Ford	D	2
46	Micra	N04	Nissan	A	4
52	Mondeo	F01	Ford	C	10
52	E190	M02	Mercedes Benz	D	2
57	C230	M02	Mercedes Benz	E	2
63	Tipo	F02	Fiat	B	3
			Total cars authorised		45

Figure 3-8 Example report from EU-Rent: Authorised Car Stocks

In this example, the report contains some non-repeating data about the Branch which is level 1 and some repeating data which is level 2. This can be represented, either as an indented list or a diagram. The indented list is as follows:

      1   Branch Information

          2   Stock Information.

If thought useful the levels may be illustrated in a structured diagram as shown in Figure 3-9.

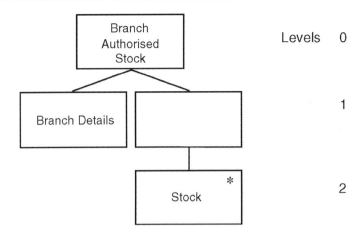

Figure 3-9 Structured diagram showing structure of data

In this example, the box 'Branch Details' describes the EU-Rent Branch from which rentals are made and the box 'Stock' describes cars of a given model at a branch.

The un-normalised relation derived from this source, annotated with the level of each attribute, is as follows:

Branch	**Level**
Branch ID	1
Branch Name	1
Branch Address	1
Model ID	2
Model Name	2
Manufacturer ID	2
Manufacturer Name	2
Car Group	2
Number Authorised	2

Note that Total Cars Authorised is not listed as an attribute, because it can be calculated from other items on the report. In analysing inputs and outputs using Relational Data Analysis, it is a generally accepted convention that derived data is excluded from the analysis. For example, totals at the bottom of reports are derived for the purpose of the reports and do not generally have any persistence within the system. The reason for excluding derived data is that it introduces redundancy into the data – if the elements used to calculate the derived data items are present, there is no need to store the derived result as it can be recalculated when required. However, this should not be treated as a hard-and-fast rule. For example, in a banking system, an account balance is derivable as it can be re-calculated at any time by looking through all the transactions for that account. This is ignoring the fact that the account balance is an important item of data to the users and would represent an enormous processing overhead to implement in this way. A reasonable rule of thumb is to ignore derivable data, for example totals at the bottom of reports. All other derivable items should be treated as real data.

The next task is to choose a key for the un-normalised relation. Any attribute can be chosen for this purpose but it is better to choose a 'sensible' key by following these guidelines:

- the key should have a unique value for each row;

- the key should not repeat within a single row;

- choose the smallest number of attributes;

- choose numeric keys rather than alphabetic keys.

Figure 3-10 shows the un-normalised relation for the form from Figure 3-8 with the keys and repeating groups indicated:

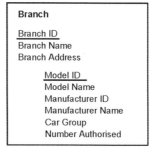

Figure 3-10 Example of un-normalised relations

3.3.4 Convert to First Normal Form (1NF)

The next stage in Relational Data Analysis is to convert the un-normalised data into First Normal Form (1NF) by the separating out of any repeating groups of data items (nested relations). A repeating group is defined as:

> *A single data item or group of data items within the relation that may occur with multiple values for a single value of the primary key.*

The analyst represents first level repeating groups (nested relations) as separate relations, copying the primary key of the outer relation to the inner one, to form part of a compound or hierarchic key. The resultant normalised form is commonly referred to as First Normal Form.

The un-normalised relation 'Branch' described above is converted into First Normal Form is shown in Figure 3-11:

Learning Resources
Centre

Branch	Stock
<u>Branch ID</u>	<u>Branch ID</u>
Branch Name	<u>Model ID</u>
Branch Address	Model Name
	Manufacturer ID
	Manufacturer Name
	Car Group
	Number Authorised

Figure 3-11 Example of First Normal Form

Note that the primary keys in these relations may in fact contain redundancy (i.e., not all the attributes may be required). The redundant attributes in the primary key are removed in a later activity when the dependencies are considered

3.3.5 Convert to Second Normal Form (2NF)

The next step is to convert the First Normal Form relations into Second Normal Form. This is carried out by removing part-key dependencies. Only those relations with compound keys need be examined. This process is carried out in two activities, the first is an optimisation which avoids trivial examples being considered in the second activity:

- Remove any redundant attributes from the primary key;

- Remove attributes not fully dependent on the primary key.

Remove any redundant attributes from the primary key

Where a key consists of several attributes, each attribute should be considered in turn to evaluate whether the key would still be unique if it were to be excluded. In other words, look for the smallest number of attributes or minimum sufficient key. If an attribute is found to be unnecessary, it should be dropped from the primary key but retained as an attribute of the relation.

Remove attributes not fully dependent on the primary key

For each non-key attribute in the relation, the question to ask here is "Does this data item depend on the whole of the primary key or only part of it?"

When partial key dependencies are identified in a relation, the attributes involved are moved to a new relation the key of which is that part of the key upon which the attributes were dependent. For the 1NF relations shown above, this activity results in the following relations:

```
Branch               Stock                Model

Branch ID            Branch ID            Model ID
Branch Name          Model ID             Model Name
Branch Address       Number Authorised    Manufacturer ID
                                          Manufacturer Name
                                          Car Group
```

Figure 3-12 Example of Second Normal Form

Here, the attributes which are dependent upon the Model ID only are moved to a separate relation (Model) with a key of Model ID.

3.3.6 Convert to Third Normal Form (3NF)

In this activity, non-candidate key (inter-data) dependencies are removed. The search is for any attribute (or group of attributes), which is not already identified as a candidate key, on which some other attribute is fully dependent.

To identify attributes which are not identified as candidate keys but which have other attributes dependent upon them, it is necessary to examine successive possible combinations of attributes in each relation to determine the dependency relationships between them.

The following are the activities that should be undertaken to ensure the relations are in Third Normal Form:

- identify any non-candidate key dependencies;

- partition any relations not in 3NF.

These are explained further below.

Identify any non-candidate key dependencies

For any two non-key attributes A and B the questions to ask are:

- 'Given a value for A, is there only one possible value for B?'.

If such an attribute B is found to be dependent upon attribute A:

- 'Is attribute A a candidate key?'

The reason for asking these two questions is to identify inter-data dependencies which may lead to the identification of new relations.

The first question will lead to the identification of any data that is not wholly dependent upon the primary keys that have been selected so far. For example, in the Second Normal

Form relations identified for EU-Rent, the Model relation has the primary key of Model ID and the attributes Model Name, Manufacturer ID, Manufacturer Name and Car Group. By examining these attributes, it can be seen that Manufacturer ID and Manufacturer Name are linked in some way that is independent of Model. For each value of Manufacturer ID, there will be only one value of Manufacturer Name.

The second question should be asked before any action is taken to separate out these items. If it was found that there was any inter-data dependency upon an attribute that had already been identified as a candidate key for the Second Normal Form relation, it would have been ignored as this dependency is already covered by the primary key of the relation. For example, if there was a Car relation with a primary key of Registration Number with an attribute of Body Number (a candidate key for Car), it is likely that a number of dependencies would be identified, linking all attributes of Car to Body Number as well as Registration Number. This does not identify any new dependencies – the dependencies have already been explored when a primary key was selected.

In this case the answer to the second question for the Manufacturer ID discussed above is 'no': Manufacturer ID is not a candidate key for Model.

Partition any relations not in 3NF

The dependent attribute is moved to a separate relation with the attributes) upon which it depends as its primary key. The attributes which form this new primary key are not removed from the original relation. Instead, they are marked as a foreign key (usually with an asterisk).

In the example above, it is not clear whether Manufacturer ID or Manufacturer Name is the dependent attribute and which should be the new key. A choice is made on the basis of which attribute is likely to be non-changeable. Manufacturer's names can be changed whereas a Manufacturer ID is assigned by the EU-Rent system and can therefore be constrained to be non-changeable. Manufacturer ID is therefore chosen as the primary key of the new relation as shown below:

Branch	**Stock**	**Model**	**Manufacturer**
Branch ID	Branch ID	Model ID	Manufacturer ID
Branch Name	Model ID	Model Name	Manufacturer Name
Branch Address	Number Authorised	* Manufacturer ID	
		Car Group	

Figure 3-13 Example of Third Normal Form

Note that the key of Manufacturer remains in Model as a foreign key and that the key Model ID remains as part of the compound key in Stock.

3.3.7 Rationalise results

Consider combining relations with identical primary keys and dropping redundant relations. The order of attributes is not significant.

Note that in practice, the names used for the resulting relations would in general be the names from the Logical Data Model for the entities corresponding to the relations.

If many relations have been combined together then it may be useful to reapply the Third Normal Form Analysis to check that the combined relations are still in true Third Normal Form.

The completed RDA analysis is illustrated in the Working Paper for this example in Figure 3-14.

UNF	Level	1NF	2NF	3NF	Relation Name
Branch ID	1	Branch ID	Branch ID	Branch ID	BRANCH
Branch Name	1	Branch Name	Branch Name	Branch Name	
Branch Address	1	Branch Address	Branch Address	Branch Address	
Model ID	2				
Model Name	2	Branch ID	Branch ID	Branch ID	STOCK
Manufacturer ID	2	Model ID	Model ID	Model ID	
Manufacturer Name	2	Model Name	Number Authorised	Number Authorised	
Car Group	2	Manufacturer ID			
Number Authorised	2	Manufacturer Name			
		Car Group	Model ID	Model ID	MODEL
		Number Authorised	Model Name	Model Name	
			Manufacturer ID	* Manufacturer ID	
			Manufacturer Name	Car Group	
			Car Group		
				Manufacturer ID	MANUFACTURER
				Manufacturer Name	

Figure 3-14 Completed RDA Working paper

3.3.8 Convert Third Normal Form Relations into partial Logical Data Models

Normalised relations and Logical Data Models are two different ways of modelling similar information. Entities in a Logical Data Model correspond to 3NF relations and similarly the relationships in a Logical Data Model equate to the candidate key/foreign key correspondences of 3NF.

The basic activities for creating a Logical Data Model from named 3NF relations are as follows:

- Create an entity for each of the 3NF data relations;

- Mark the qualifying elements of hierarchic keys as foreign keys;

- Check that all the masters of compound and hierarchic key relations are present;

- Make compound key relations into details;
- Make relations with foreign keys into details;
- Add the attributes for the derived entities.

Create an entity for each data relation

In practice, this means that each relation is assigned a box. It can be helpful if all key (primary and foreign) attributes are listed inside the box.

Some of the Third Normal Form relations that have been derived for the EU-Rent System are as follows:

Branch	**Manufacturer**	**Model**
Branch ID	Manufacturer ID	Model ID
Branch Name	Manufacturer Name	* Manufacturer ID
Branch Address		Car Group
Stock	**Car**	**Car Booking**
Branch ID	Registration Number	(Registration Number)
Model ID	* Model ID	(Booking Number)
Number Authorised	Colour	Booking Start Date
	Purchase Date	Booking End Date
		Pick-Up Time
		Return Time

Figure 3-15 Third Normal Form Relations

Each of these relations is placed in a box indicating the primary and foreign keys as shown in Figure 3-16.

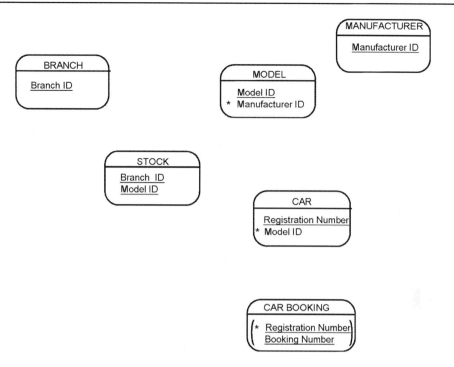

Figure 3-16 First activity of converting Third Normal Form Relations into a Logical Data Model

Note: it is useful if the boxes are laid out such that the next four rules can be implemented without creating a confusing maze of linkages. The Required System Logical Data Model will give guidance on this since most relations will be recognisable as Logical Data Model entities.

Mark the qualifying elements of hierarchic keys as foreign keys

If the entire primary key of a relation is a hierarchic key, mark the higher level, qualifying element (or elements) as a foreign key. Do not treat this type of relation as a compound key relation when using the following rules.

There is only one hierarchic key in the example above: Car Booking has a hierarchic key of Registration Number and Booking Number. The upper element of the key is Registration Number and this is marked as a foreign key as shown in Figure 3-17.

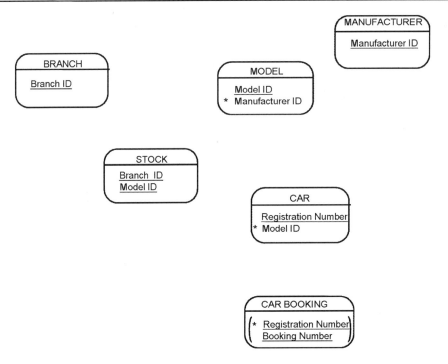

Figure 3-17 Second activity of converting Third Normal Form Relations into a Logical Data Model

Check that all the masters of compound key relations are present

Check that each element of every compound key occurs as the simple or hierarchic key of another relation. If an element is part of a compound key, but is not the sole key of another data group then:

- create a new relation with the element as its key;

- make this new data group a master of each data group which has the elements as part of its compound key;

- mark it as a foreign key in all other relations where it appears as a non-key element.

In the example shown in Figure 3-17, the only compound key is the key to Stock which is Branch ID/Model ID. Both of these elements are present as simple keys of other entities, so no action needs to be taken.

Make compound key relations into details

Make compound key relations the details of those relations that have either a single or multiple element of the compound as their total primary key. In the example shown above, this means that Branch and Model are both masters of Stock. This is shown in Figure 3-18.

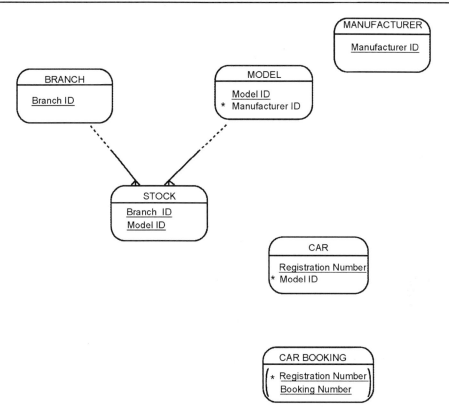

Figure 3-18 Fourth activity of converting Third Normal Form Relations into a Logical Data Model

Please note that the optionality of the relationships in this and subsequent diagrams cannot be determined simply by examination of RDA relations. The relationship which is optional from the master and mandatory from the detail is a 'default'. All relationship optionality is determined by comparison with the Logical Data Model, by examination of the data. Also, relationships are not usually labelled during the construction of sub-models from RDA relations unless there are multiple relationships between the same pair of entities.

It is possible to allocate multiple elements of a detail's compound key to a single master. Each element must be allocated only once. This is illustrated by a generalised example in Figure 3-19.

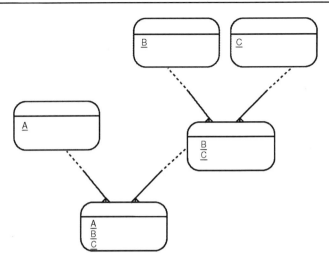

Figure 3-19 Multiple elements of key assigned to a single master

In this example, a relation with a key of A/B/C is assigned to relations with keys A and B/C rather than to the three masters with individual elements of the key.

Make relations with foreign keys into details

Make a relation with a foreign key the detail of the relation that has the key as its total primary key.

This is demonstrated in Figure 3-20.

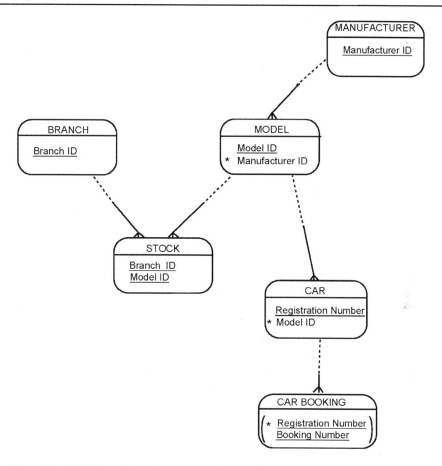

Figure 3-20 Fifth activity of converting 3NF Relations into a Logical Data Model

In this example,

- Car is made a master of Car Booking as Registration Number has been marked as a foreign key;

- Model is made master of Car and Manufacturer is made master of Model.

In order to minimise the number of relationships, it is permissible to regard multiple foreign keys within a single relation as a foreign compound key.

Considerations in the conversion of Third Normal Form Relations into a Logical Data Model

The activities described above are demonstrated here with reference to a simple example where all relationships are one-to-many between different relations. There are a number of situations which may be encountered which are not as straightforward and require additional guidance. These situations are briefly described in the following paragraphs.

One-to-one Relationships

If two relations contain foreign keys which point to one another (i.e. each one has the other ones primary key marked as a foreign key), this may identify a one-to-one relationship. Often in examples of one-to-one relationships, investigation will reveal that the participation of one of the entities in the relationship is optional.

Recursive relationships

Recursive ('pigs ear') relationships occur when a relation has a foreign key that references the same relation.

Multiple relationships

It is possible for there to be more than one relationship between a pair of entities, or between an entity and itself. Such multiple relationships are identified by the existence of multiple foreign keys to the same relation in different roles. This will be difficult to spot by applying the principles of Relational Data Analysis as any multiple attributes are likely to have been merged. Care should be taken during rationalisation that attributes are not merged if they are assuming different roles.

Deriving attributes of entities from relations

In general the rules for deriving the attributes of an entity corresponding to a relation are quite simple. The attributes of the entity are all the attributes of the relation.

3.3.9 Compare the Relational Data Analysis models with the Logical Data Model

The model derived through Relational Data Analysis is compared with the Logical Data Model. This will highlight any errors or omissions in the Logical Data Model. Before any changes are made to the Logical Data model, these should be checked to ensure that requirements for enquiries can still be met.

The model derived through RDA should be compared with the Logical Data model in the following way:

- entities on the Logical Data Model should be compared with relations. Ideally, there should be a one-to-one correspondence between entities and relations. Where there is a mis-match, the Logical Data Model may need to be updated to match the results of RDA. Note that models developed using RDA are unlikely to contain entity aspects or sub/super-types;

- relationships between entities should be compared with relationships between relations. It is likely that the RDA model will not contain much of the optionality and exclusivity found on the Logical Data Model. However, if the relationships identified during RDA are between relations which are not connected as entities on the Logical Data Model, changes may need to be made to the Logical Data Model;

- attributes within relations should be checked against attributes in entities. Where new attributes are identified in relations, the analyst should consider adding them into the entities or ensuring that the information is available within other attributes. If strict naming conventions are adopted then this will ensure that the names of attributes derived through Relational Data Analysis are easily cross-checked to those identified as part of Logical Data Modelling.

3.4 Worked Example of Relational Data Analysis

The steps of Relational Data Analysis are demonstrated here with reference to a report which is required in the new system which lists stocks of cars at a particular branch. An example of the report layout is given in Figure 3-21.

Branch	357	London	North				9-Sep-94
Group	Model		Manufacturer	Auth			
A	41	Uno	Fiat	4	Registration	Colour	Purchase Date
					K123 RDA	Red	14-Jul-93
					L336TNF	White	21-Sep-93
					L235LDM	White	12-Oct-93
					M998ECD	Black	4-Aug-94
	46	Micra	Nissan	6	Registration	Colour	Purchase Date
					L987ELH	White	12-Dec-93
					L775ECD	White	17-Jan-94
					L776ECD	Blue	17-Jan-94
					Purch Ref	Quantity	Delivery Date
					123456	2	16-Sep-94
					123463	1	2-Oct-94
B	26	Escort	Ford	12	Registration	Colour	Purchase Date
					L556EPM	Black	16-Dec-93
					L456TNF	Red	26-Jan-94
					L221LDM	Red	2-Feb-94
					L222LDM	Blue	2-Feb-94
					L223LDM	Black	2-Feb-94
					M676ECD	White	4-Sep-94
					Purch Ref	Quantity	Delivery Date
					123451	4	29-Sep-94
					123451	2	12-Oct-94

Figure 3-21 Example Report used as an input to Relational Data Analysis

This is a fairly complicated report and contains a number of 'levels' which can be represented thus:

1   Branch Information

      2   Car Group Information

          3   Stock Information

               4   Car Information
               4   Delivery Information

The terms used here are explained as follows:

- **Group**. Car Group for which a rental tariff is defined;
- **Stock**. Cars of a given model at a branch: includes recommended number, actual cars owned by branch and number of cars on order;
- **Car**. Car owned by EU-Rent's rental business;
- **Delivery**. Number of cars of a given model ordered by the EU-Rent purchasing system, to be delivered to a branch on or about a specified delivery date.

A more graphical representation of the levels within this report is shown in Figure 3-22.

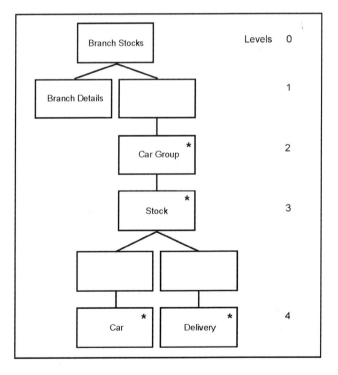

Figure 3-22 Graphical representation of data on Relational Data Analysis source

The un-normalised relation, together with its level, is listed in the left -hand column of the Relational Data Analysis Working Paper as shown in Figure 3-23.

UNF	Level	1NF	2NF	3NF	Relation Name
Branch ID	1				
Branch Name	1				
Group Code	2				
Model ID	3				
Model Name	3				
Manufacturer Name	3				
Number Authorised	3				
Registration Number	4				
Colour	4				
Purchase Date	4				
Delivery ID	4				
Purchase Ref	4				
Delivery Quantity	4				
Delivery Date	4				

Figure 3-23 Un-normalised form listed on Relational Data Analysis Working Paper

Each repeating group is uniquely identified by a combination of the key of the level above and the key of the repeating group. This means that the level 1 identifier is Branch ID, the level 2 identifier is Branch ID and Group Code and so on.

By comparing this example with the original form, it may be seen that an attribute, Delivery ID, has been added to the un-normalised relation which does not correspond directly to any data item on the original report. Delivery ID has been introduced as an implied attribute. The report has a repeating line, of Purchase Ref, Quantity and Delivery Date. By looking at the report (or more importantly conferring with users) it is determined that none of these items is a unique identifier – each can have the same value appearing more than once for different values of the other two items. In order to have a unique identifier for each group of Purchase Ref /Quantity/Delivery Date, this requires the introduction of the implied attribute Delivery ID which is arbitrarily assigned a unique value for each line on the report within model to distinguish different deliveries for a specific model.

Convert to First Normal Form

Conversion of the un-normalised form to First Normal Form (1NF) is relatively mechanical. This step involves separating out repeating groups and copying down the identifiers from higher levels to lower levels in the hierarchy to provide a unique key for each group. No account is taken, at this stage, of the fact that all items in a repeating group may not require all parts of the key as their identifier. First Normal Form is simply a starting point and concentrates only on separating out repeating groups.

The '1NF' column of the Relational Data Analysis Working Paper is completed as shown in Figure 3-24.

UNF	Level	1NF	2NF	3NF	Relation Name
Branch ID	1	Branch ID			
Branch Name	1	Branch Name			
Group Code	2				
Model ID	3	Branch ID			
Model Name	3	Group Code			
Manufacturer Name	3				
Number Authorised	3	Branch ID			
Registration Number	4	Group Code			
Colour	4	Model ID			
Purchase Date	4	Model Name			
Delivery ID	4	Manufacturer Name			
		Number Authorised			
Purchase Ref	4				
Delivery Quantity	4				
Delivery Date	4				
		Branch ID			
		Group Code			
		Model ID			
		Registration Number			
		Colour			
		Purchase Date			
		(Branch ID)			
		(Group Code)			
		(Model ID)			
		(Delivery ID)			
		Purchase Ref			
		Delivery Quantity			
		Delivery Date			

Figure 3-24 First Normal Form listed on Relational Data Analysis Working Paper

The relation containing the identifier Delivery ID has been distinguished from the others by a series of brackets around all elements of the key. This is to denote the key as being hierarchic (composite) meaning that Delivery ID is only unique if taken in combination with all the other items in the key enclosed by brackets. This acts as a reminder that Delivery ID should not be separated out from these other elements of the key or it will cease to be unique. As it stands, there is some redundancy in the First Normal Form relations which can be removed as shown in Figure 3-25.

1NF	1NF (redundancy removed)
<u>Branch ID</u> Branch Name	<u>Branch ID</u> Branch Name
<u>Branch ID</u> <u>Group Code</u>	<u>Branch ID</u> <u>Group Code</u>
<u>Branch ID</u> <u>Group Code</u> <u>Model ID</u> Model Name Manufacturer Name Number Authorised	<u>Branch ID</u> Group Code <u>Model ID</u> Model Name Manufacturer Name Number Authorised
<u>Branch ID</u> <u>Group Code</u> <u>Model ID</u> <u>Registration</u> <u>Number</u> Colour Purchase Date	Branch ID Group Code Model ID <u>Registration</u> <u>Number</u> Colour Purchase Date
<u>(Branch ID)</u> <u>(Group Code)</u> <u>(Model ID)</u> <u>(Delivery ID)</u> Purchase Ref Delivery Quantity Delivery Date	<u>(Branch ID)</u> Group Code <u>(Model ID)</u> <u>(Delivery ID)</u> Purchase Ref Delivery Quantity Delivery Date

Figure 3-25 Removing redundancy from the First Normal Form relation

In Figure 3-25, some elements of the keys have been demoted to being attributes as they are not required to determine unique values for other attributes. This demonstrates the principle of looking for the minimum set of attributes needed for a primary key. For example, the attributes of the relation with the key of Branch ID/Group Code/Model ID and Delivery ID are all uniquely identified without Group Code so this is dropped from the hierarchic key resulting in a relation with the hierarchic (composite) key of Branch ID/Model ID/Delivery ID.

It should be stressed that the analyst, in conjunction with the user, is responsible for the choice of implied keys. In this example, it might have been possible to identify a Delivery ID that was unique throughout the system, in which case there would be no need for a hierarchic key. However, there was no guarantee that the assignment of values to occurrences of Delivery ID could be controlled sufficiently to ensure that each value would be unique. The choice was made, therefore, to select an identifier that could be controlled sufficiently to ensure unique values for keys.

Convert to Second Normal Form

The transformation from First Normal Form to Second Normal Form is carried out by removing part-key dependencies. Only multi-part keys are considered at this stage - relations with simple keys are copied across unchanged from First Normal Form to Second Normal Form.

To convert First Normal Form relations into Second Normal Form relations, all attributes in the relation are checked to determine whether they are dependent upon the whole key or only part of the key. This involves checking the different parts of the key to discover interdependencies between them.

The '2NF' column of the Relational Data Analysis Working Paper is completed as shown in Figure 3-26 (note that the First Normal Form relations with redundancy removed have been used here).

UNF	Level	1NF	2NF	3NF	Relation Name
Branch ID	1	Branch ID	Branch ID		
Branch Name	1	Branch Name	Branch Name		
Group Code	2				
Model ID	3	Branch ID	Branch ID		
Model Name	3	Group Code	Group Code		
Manufacturer Name	3				
Number Authorised	3	Branch ID	Branch ID		
Registration	4	Group Code	Model ID		
Number		Model ID	Number		
Colour	4	Model Name	Authorised		
		Manufacturer			
Purchase Date	4	Name			
Delivery ID	4	Number	Model ID		
		Authorised	Group Code		
Purchase Ref	4		Model Name		
			Manufacturer		
Delivery Quantity	4		Name		
Delivery Date	4				
		Branch ID	Registration		
			Number		
		Group Code	Branch ID		
		Model ID	Model ID		
		Registration	Group Code		
		Number			
		Colour	Colour		
		Purchase Date	Purchase Date		
		(Branch ID)	(Branch ID)		
		Group Code	(Model ID)		
		(Model ID)	(Delivery ID)		
		(Delivery ID)	Purchase Ref		
		Purchase Ref	Delivery Quantity		
		Delivery Quantity	Delivery Date		
		Delivery Date			
			Model ID		
			Group Code		

Figure 3-26 Second Normal Form listed on Relational Data Analysis Working Paper

In this example, the first two relations have been carried across unchanged. The first relation has only a simple key and the second has no further interdependencies to identify. The relation with the key of Branch ID/Model ID is split into two relations:

- the Number Authorised is found to be uniquely identified by a combination of Branch ID and Model ID so it has been retained in the relation with Branch ID and Model ID as keys;

- Model Name and Manufacturer Name are specific to the model of the car and are independent of the branch. Therefore, Model Name and Manufacturer Name are put into a relation with Model ID as the key;

- the Group Code is also found to be uniquely identified by the Model ID so it is put into the relation with Model ID as the simple key (this relation is also identified from looking at the relation with a hierarchic key of Branch ID/Model ID/Delivery ID).

Convert to Third Normal Form

To transform the Second Normal Form relations into Third Normal Form, inter-data dependencies are investigated. The result of this exercise on the example above is shown in Figure 3-27.

UNF	Level	1NF	2NF	3NF	Relation Name
		Branch ID Branch Name	Branch ID Branch Name	Branch ID Branch Name	BRANCH
Branch ID	1				
Branch Name	1				
Group Code	2	Branch ID Group Code	Branch ID Group Code	Branch ID Group Code	BRANCH/GROUP AVAILABILITY
Model ID	3				
Model Name	3				
Manufacturer Name	3	Branch ID	Branch ID	Branch ID	STOCK
Number Authorised	3	Group Code	Model ID	Model ID	
Registration	4	Model ID	Number	Number	
Number		Model Name	Authorised	Authorised	
Colour	4	Manufacturer			
Purchase Date	4	Name	Model ID	Model ID	MODEL
		Number	Model Name	Model Name	
Delivery ID	4	Authorised	Group Code	*Group Code	
			Manufacturer	* Manufacturer ID	
Purchase Ref	4		Name		
Delivery Quantity	4				
				Manufacturer ID	
Delivery Date	4			Manufacturer Name	MANUFACTURER
		Branch ID	Registration Number	Registration Number	CAR
		Group Code	Branch ID	* Branch ID	
		Model ID	Model ID	* Model ID	
		Registration Number	Group Code	Colour	
		Colour	Colour	Purchase Date	
		Purchase Date	Purchase Date		
				Model ID *Group Code	MODEL
		(Branch ID)	(Branch ID)	(Branch ID)	
		Group Code	(Model ID)	(Model ID)	DELIVERY
		(Model ID)	(Delivery ID)	(Delivery ID)	
		(Delivery ID)	Purchase Ref	Purchase Ref	
		Purchase Ref	Delivery Quantity	Delivery Quantity	
		Delivery Quantity	Delivery Date	Delivery Date	
		Delivery Date			
			Model ID Group Code	Model ID *Group Code	MODEL

Figure 3-27 Relational Data Analysis: Third Normal Form

Note: The lines across the grid are here used to indicate the derivation of the normal form relations. They can be used if thought useful but should not be regarded as mandatory.

Here, the majority of relations remain unchanged. However, the relation with Manufacturer Name as an attribute has been rationalised based on an understanding of the data. Manufacturer ID is introduced as a primary key for Manufacturer Name. This is done because the analyst has recognised that Manufacturer Name should not remain in the relation identified by Model ID and has required it to be removed from the relation and referenced by a foreign key. We can use only primary keys as foreign keys in other relations, and Manufacturer Name is not a primary key. This requires the introduction of Manufacturer ID.

By examining the attributes of the relations and comparing them to the keys of other relations, several more foreign keys are identified as shown above, for example, Branch ID and Model ID are shown as attributes of the relation with Registration Number as primary key but they are both used as keys of other relations. They are therefore marked as foreign keys.

Some tentative names have been entered into the Relation Name column to indicate the relations that will be compared directly with entities on the Logical Data Model. At this stage, the relations have not yet been rationalised and these names will be subject to change.

Rationalise results

Rationalisation involves comparing the Third Normal Form relations that have been derived by applying the Relational Data Analysis rules to groupings of data. This can be done on a source-by-source basis, for a group of Relational Data Analysis sources or for all results of Relational Data Analysis. The more sources used for comparison the better will be the results: relationships between data that appear in one context should be validated by relationships that appear in another context. Groupings of data organised for presentation to the user will not necessarily provide all data needed to form full relations.

If relations have been identified that have the same primary key, consideration should be given to merging them. In doing this, care should be taken in comparing the attributes of the merged relations. For example, if a date appears in two different relations which are merged, examine the dates carefully to see if they are the same or different dates. If two relations are merged they are potentially back in Second Normal Form and should be checked accordingly.

The 3NF results above, combined with the results of other Relational Data Analysis exercises undertaken on other selected EU-Rent sources, rationalise into the following relations:

Branch

Branch ID
Branch Name
Branch Address

Branch/Group Availability

Branch ID
Group Code

Manufacturer

Manufacturer ID
Manufacturer Name

Stock
Branch ID
Model ID
Number Authorised

Model
Model ID
Group Code
Model Name
*Manufacturer ID

Customer
Driver Id
Customer Name

Car
Registration Number
*Branch ID
*Model ID
Colour
Purchase Date

Delivery
(Branch ID)
(Model ID)
(Delivery ID)
Purchase Ref
Delivery Quantity
Delivery Date

Rental
Rental ID
*Branch ID
Start Date
End Date
*Driver Id

Figure 3-28 Rationalised results from Relational Data Analysis

One of the results of this is that key of Branch ID/Group Code does not appear to have any attributes and does not appear to be a useful grouping. It is also difficult to find a meaningful name that describes this grouping. After careful consideration, this relation is dropped altogether. This means that although Group Code was selected as a key at the beginning of Relational Data Analysis, it has turned out to be a non-key attribute of Model, based on the analysis of the sources seen so far.

Convert Third Normal Form relations into partial Logical Data Models

The conversion of the 3NF relations into a partial Logical Data Model is relatively mechanistic. Figure 3-29 shows the partial Logical Data Structure that was derived from the relations shown above.

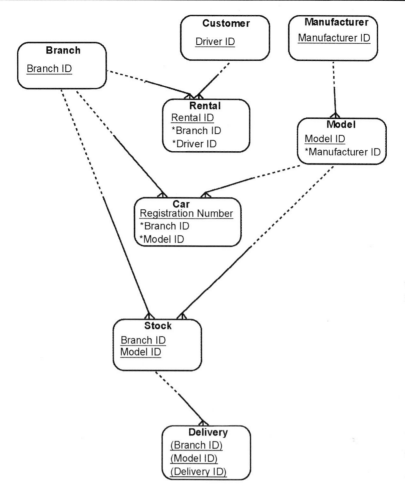

Figure 3-29 Partial Logical Data Structure constructed from relations

This example demonstrates the following principles:

- relations containing foreign keys have been made details of the entities with the foreign keys as their primary keys. This applies to relationships between the following:

    - Rental is made a detail of Customer and Branch;

    - Model is made a detail of Manufacturer;

    - Car is made a detail of Model and Branch;

- relations with a multi-part primary key have been made a detail of relations which have individual parts of the multi-part key as their primary keys. This applies to the following:

    - Stock is made a detail of Model and Branch (in this case, the key is compound as all parts of the key are keys of other entities);

- Delivery is made a detail of Stock (in this case the key is hierarchic as Delivery ID is unique only when qualified by the key of its master).

Before being compared with the Logical Data Model, this model requires some rationalisation. There is a 'double V' structure between Model and Branch – both Stock and Car relations have both Branch and Model as their master. By considering these relationships further, it becomes clear that Car must become a detail of Stock as shown in Figure 3-30 (Note that this relationship may already have been identified by analysis of the keys before the initial diagram was drawn.)

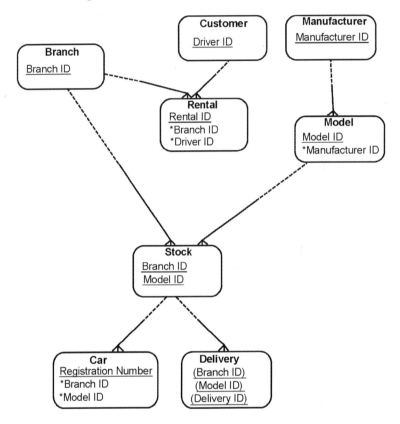

Figure 3-30 Rationalised sub-model based on Third Normal Form relations

Compare the Relational Data Analysis models with the Logical Data Model

The comparison of the Relational Data Analysis sub-models with the Logical Data Model may highlight discrepancies between the entities and relations in terms of their relationship and attributes. Some relations may exist that do not correspond to entities and vice versa.

Here, the EU-Rent Required System Logical Data Model is compared with the sub-model shown in Figure 3-30. The Logical Data Model is shown in Figure 3-31.

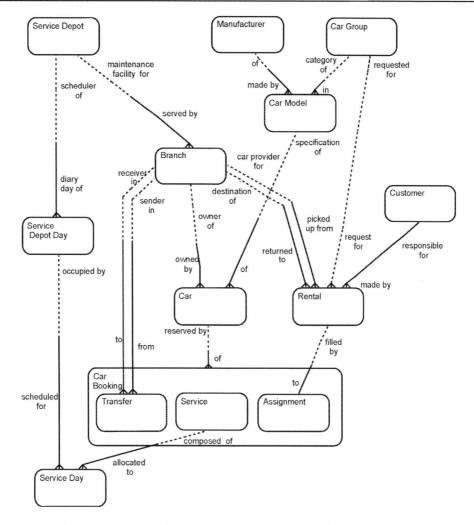

Figure 3-31 EU-Rent Required System Logical Data Model

The comparison highlights the following:

- Stock is represented as a relation but does not appear on the Logical Data Model. The attribute of Stock is Number Authorised which does not appear on the Logical Data Model. This needs further investigation – possibly resulting in the inclusion of Stock as an entity on the Logical Data Model;

- there is only one relationship between Rental and Branch on the Relational Data Analysis sub-model but two relationships between the same two entities on the Logical Data Model. This may be because the second occurrence of the foreign key to branch was rationalised out where two occurrences should have remained with different roles, or it may be because none of the Relational Data Analysis sources examined dealt with one-way rentals. In this case, the Logical Data Model is correct and is unchanged;

- Delivery appears on the Relational Data Analysis sub-model but not on the Logical Data Model. This is because this could be derived by examining each occurrence of the Car entity if required. A decision needs to be made as to whether this constitutes 'derived data' and excluded from the Logical Data Model or whether it should be included in the Logical Data Model for clarity (this trade-off is discussed above).

3.5   Relationship with other analysis and design techniques

The techniques listed below are all covered within the publications that are part of this series.

3.5.1 Logical Data Modelling (see Chapter 2)

Relational Data Analysis is a complementary technique to Logical Data Modelling and supports it as a supplementary approach to identifying and specifying information requirements.

Entity analysis derives a Logical Data Model in a top-down manner by a process of decomposition, whereas Relational Data Analysis derives a data model in a bottom-up manner by synthesising individual data items into larger data groups.

The benefits of the two data analysis techniques in combination are as follows:

- Logical Data Modelling, working essentially from the top down, ensures that the overall perception of what is important to the project in terms of data is not lost;

- Relational Data Analysis, working essentially from the bottom up, ensures that all the low-level detail is captured.

3.5.2 Data Flow Modelling (covered in the Function Modelling volume)

Data Flow Modelling can be used to provide sources for Relational Data Analysis This is achieved by examining the flows on the Data Flow Model which cross the system boundary.

3.5.3 User Object Modelling (covered in the User Centred Design volume)

The User Object Model can be used to provide candidate sources for relational Data Analysis.

4   FURTHER DATA MODELLING CONSIDERATIONS

This chapter contains extra detail about different areas of Data Modelling. It is organised into the following sections:

- More on Entities

- More on Relationship

- More on Drawing the Logical Data Model

- Presenting the Logical Data Model to users

- Logical Data Modelling and the Corporate Data Model

- Fourth and Fifth Normal Form

Although this chapter is primarily concerned with Logical Data Modelling much of the advice would also be of use in Relational Data Analysis – especially when constructing the Partial Models and when comparing the Partial Models with the Logical Data Model.

These 'extra' sections may prove useful to analysts when trying to resolve problems with the Logical Data Model.

4.1   More on Entities

4.1.1 Entity aspects – alternative approaches

Entity aspects are 'views' of a real-world entity, each of which co-exists with all other views of the same entity. The basic approach and notation for entity aspects is given in chapter 2. There the 'basic' aspect is shown as well as the aspects representing the different, 'views' of the entity in different contexts.

An example of aspects which shows this 'basic' aspect taken from the EU- Rent case study is shown in Figure 4-1. In this example, three different views of Service Depot with different behaviours are:

- as a basic aspect which represents a geographical location with an address;

- as a car maintenance provider with defined capacity (equipment and manpower), to which car service and repair work is allocated;

- as premises that need to be maintained, furnished and decorated and on which rent and property taxes need to be paid.

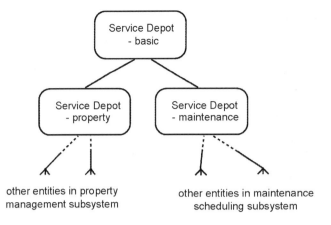

Figure 4-1 Example of entity aspects

We have taken the 'location with an address' view as the basic existence of a Service Depot and defined one-to-one relationships between it and each

of the more specific aspects. Two points to note are:

- aspects are not subtypes; an instance of a service depot has all three aspects – it is simultaneously a location, a maintenance provider and premises;

- identifying different aspects on a logical data model allows us to model distinct behaviours separately.

Sometimes it is convenient to simplify diagrams by merging the basic aspect with one of the more specific aspects (e.g., the one in the first subsystem that will be delivered) as shown in Figure 4-2.

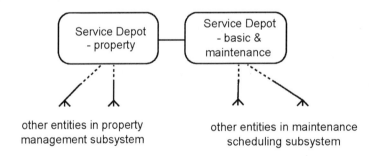

Figure 4-2 Example of merging aspects

4.1.2 Identifying sub-types

Subtypes often contain optional and mutually-exclusive attributes of the real-world entity type, but separation of common and different attributes may not be the major criterion for sub typing. Instead, sub-types could be identified by different behaviours of the same entity. For example, in the EU-Rent required system, Free Rentals and Paid Rentals are useful subtypes of the entity Rental. These sub-types are not identified because they have a few differences in attributes, but because they behave differently in that a Free Rental must be reserved in advance, the customer must be in the benefit scheme and there must be sufficient points in his or her account when the reservation is made.

Note that in some cases, sub-types may be identified which do not cover the totality of occurrences of the entity – some occurrences of the entity may simply contain the attributes listed in the super-type and have the same relationships as the super-type. Where the remaining occurrences that are not covered by specific sub-types cannot be collectively named, they can be represented by a sub-type of 'other'. A super-type does not have an independent existence from its sub-types. It is not possible to have an occurrence of the super-type without it being one of the sub-types.

4.1.3 Orthogonal sub-types

The differentiation has been made between aspects and sub-types as the fact that aspects can co-exist whereas sub-types are mutually exclusive.

One of the potential problems with identifying sub-types is that occasionally a super-type can be sub-typed in several different ways, each of which is independent of the others. For example, in the EU-Rent system, the entity Rental can be sub-typed as 'Out and Back' and 'One-way' or 'Walk-in' and 'Advance Booking'. If the strictly hierarchical form of sub-typing is used, it would be necessary to decide which sub-type comes first and then split both subtypes into the orthogonal sub-types as shown in Figure 4-3.

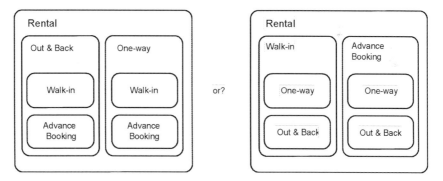

Figure 4-3 Orthogonal sub-types as a hierarchy

If there were three orthogonal sub-types, the situation would become even more difficult with all of the lowest-level sub-types needing to be sub- typed again.

To avoid this problem, it is possible to use a combination of sub-types and entity aspects. In the EU-Rent example, two aspects can be identified for the two sets of sub-types shown in Figure 4-3 and they can be sub-typed as shown in Figure 4-4.

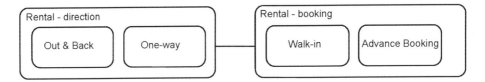

Figure 4-4 Use of aspects to represent orthogonal sub-types

4.2   More on Relationships

4.2.1 Relationship Identifiers

Although relationship identifiers must be recorded in the repository, it is often useful to suppress the obvious ones (those that are obvious from the entity names and the general context) from the diagram. The ones that are named on the diagram are then highlighted as needing special attention or understanding.

4.2.2 Recursive relationships

A hierarchic recursive relationship is usually shown as a 'pig's ear' which is fully optional. It is fully optional to indicate that the top of the hierarchy has no master and the bottom of the hierarchy has no detail. However, this is rather vague and does not give any indication of the extent of the hierarchy. It is often useful to separate out the top and/or bottom entity of the hierarchy to make this more clear and precise. This is demonstrated in Figure 4-5.

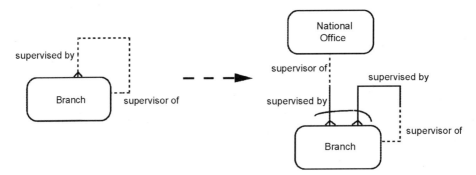

Figure 4-5 More precise hierarchical recursive relationship

In this example, the top of the hierarchy has been separated out which allows the 'pig's ear' to become mandatory at the detail end which is now in an exclusive group with the relationship to the top of the hierarchy. It is often necessary to consider the top or bottom entity of the hierarchy separately as relationships to the top or bottom are often different from layers in between.

Recursive relationships may be symmetrical or asymmetrical:

- **Symmetrical**: in EU-Rent a car model may be *substituted by* other car models, and may be a *substitute for* other car models, but it is the same set in each case - all the other models in the same car group. Sometimes we have to create a new entity to deal with this kind of relationship as shown in Figure 4-6;

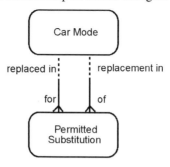

Figure 4-6: Example of symmetrical recursive relationship

- **Asymmetrical**: suppose (in a more complex system than EU-Rent) that we organised substitution model by model, without car groups, and that some substitutions were not symmetrical, so that model A could be used in place of model B, but not vice versa. We need to create a link entity, similar to that for the 'bill of materials' example. But there is no 'top' and 'bottom' of the structure. The top is whichever car group you start with and, to define the bottom, you need to specify restrictions on access. Recursion is allowed so one way of running out of network is if you encounter a car model you have already tried. You will also probably want to restrict the depth of indirect references (replacement in permitted substitution, for replacement in permitted substitution, for ...) so that you don't offer a Rolls Royce as substitute for a Fiat Panda, via a long chain of permitted substitutions.

4.2.3 Use of sub-typing to clarify optional relationships and exclusive groups

Sub-typing can be introduced in the Logical Data Model to clarify optional relationships and exclusive groups.

An example of sub-typing clarifying an optional relationship is shown in Figure 4-7.

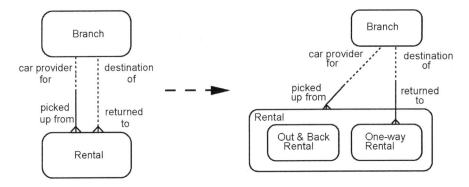

Figure 4-7 Use of sub-typing to clarify optional relationship

In this example, the second relationship between Branch and Rental is fully optional. The
only reason it is optional is that it only applies to one-way rentals. If the Rental entity is
sub-typed to distinguish one-way rentals from out-and-back rentals, the relationship can be
made mandatory to the sub-type. This is much more precise than the optional relationship
and highlights the different behaviours of the two different types of rental. Note that the
graphical notation cannot capture the restriction that (in this case) the 'returned to' branch
must be different from 'picked up from' branch. This will have to be documented elsewhere
as a restriction or 'business rule' of the system.

Sub-typing can also be used to resolve exclusive relationships. This is demonstrated in
Figure 4-8.

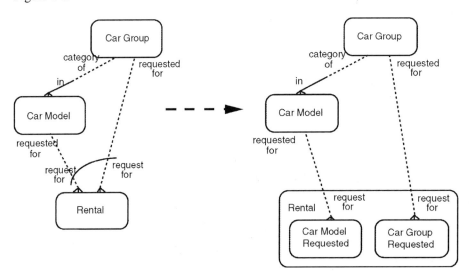

Figure 4-8 Resolution of Exclusive Group using sub-typing

In this example, the Rental has been sub-typed to show the different types of rental
indicated by the exclusive arc. It is not always necessary to resolve exclusive arcs in this
way but it can be a useful way of identifying candidate sub-types when developing the
Logical Data Model.

4.2.4 Removing redundant relationships from the Logical Data Structure

Potentially redundant relationships will be considered throughout the process of logical data modelling but particularly when developing the Required System Logical Data Model.

Since the Logical Data Model is developed to reflect the structure of the data, not all of the relationships identified may be required for functional purposes. Some relationships may actually be redundant. A redundant relationship is one which provides the same information as two or more others, derived in all circumstances from other relationships.

Redundant relationships may occur in closed loops. In its simplest form the closed loop consists of a triangular structure such as is demonstrated in the left hand structure in Figure 4-9. One of the relationships can be removed if it is redundant. However, care needs to be taken to consider the semantics before simplifying. It is not possible to determine whether a relationship is redundant simply by looking at the Logical Data Structure; an understanding of the actual occurrences is essential.

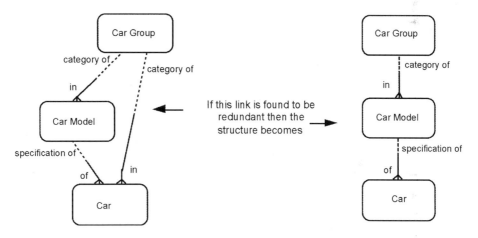

Figure 4-9 Example of redundant relationships

Note that the first structure in Figure 4-9 is actually wrong in that it implies that the entity Car can have two different relationships with Car Group – one direct and the other through Car Model.

Another potential redundancy situation occurs with what is known as 'double Vs'. Look for 'double Vs' in the structure and decide if the two link entities are related. Often they are in a 1:m relationship. These may be rationalised as shown in Figure 4-10.

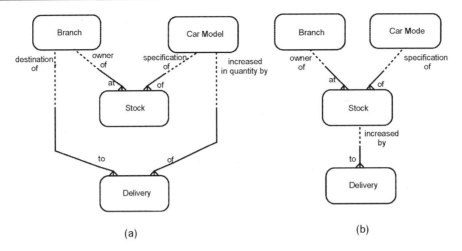

Figure 4-10 Rationalisation of 'double-V'

In this example the structure 'a' contains double Vs which, after discussion with the users, are resolved into the structure on the right – structure 'b'.

There are dangers in attempting to remove redundant relationships. A complex element of the structure to satisfy a particular requirement may be inadvertently removed. Optionality of the different relationships should be examined to ensure that after removal these have not changed. After rationalisation it is essential to validate the structure again to ensure that it satisfies known functional requirements.

4.2.5 Resolving many-to-many relationships

In the early stages of development, Logical Data Models may contain a number of many-to-many relationships reflecting the business rules of the Organisation. It may also be a convenient simplification to use m:n relationships when presenting the model to the user.

This type of relationship hides the concept of master/detail and obscures the navigation or access paths through the model. In most projects, all m:n relationships are resolved before the Required System Logical Data Model is finalised. This can be achieved by introducing a link entity which splits the relationship into two 1:m relationships.

Forcing the resolution of m:n relationships is not a mechanical process; it is a powerful analysis technique. In the majority of cases, the link entity turns out to be a genuine entity containing non-key data which provides more information about the two master entities or the nature of the relationship between them.

4.2.6 Resolving one-to-one relationships

In the early stages of development, Logical Data Models may contain a number of one-to-one relationships reflecting the business rules of the Organisation. They may also be helpful when presenting the model to the user.

Most of the relationships on the final Required System Logical Data Model will be one-to-many. All 1:1 relationships should be examined to consider one of the following courses of action:

- the two entities joined by the one-to-one relationship can be merged into one entity. Where this is done, the primary key of the new entity will usually be the primary key of one of the original entities; but if neither of those keys is satisfactory, a new key can be invented;

- the one-to-one relationship may be replaced with a one-to-many relationship (this often happens where historical occurrences of one entity are retained).

Where two entities are merged, the following may apply:

- **1:1 optional at one end**. The two entities are merged into one with optional attributes, or the optional end is made the master entity (this makes sense because this is normally the entity which is created first);

- **1:1 optional at both ends**. The analyst should check to see if there is a missing link entity via which the two entities should be related, or if one end of the relationship should be mandatory and thus treated as above. Otherwise, the two entities are merged into one with optional attributes or the entity coming into existence first should be considered the master;

- **1:1 mandatory at both ends**. A mandatory one-to-one relationship would imply that the two entities were created simultaneously. Such relationships are only valid to represent entity aspects or in exclusive groups to represent sub-type and super-type entities. In other mandatory one-to-one relationships, the two entities should be merged, unless further analysis reveals one end to be optional (and thus treated as above).

4.3   More on Drawing the Logical Data Model

4.3.1 Checking Access Paths

The Logical Data Model must provide an access path for all processes that will need to access the Logical Data Model. This is achieved by using the following read types to check that the required data can be obtained:

- read entity directly using key;

- read next detail entity of a master entity;

- read master entity of detail entity.

It is important to be sure that, as well as a link existing between entities, the structure will allow you to access the correct occurrences. An informal check on any known Access Path requirements can be undertaken at the time of constructing the Logical Data Model.

One of the most common problems encountered when checking access paths is where there is a logical discontinuity. This is where navigation is required from one entity to another via another entity which is master to both of them. In this case, it is not possible to reconcile specific occurrences of the two entities by the relationships on the Logical Data Structure as the navigation via the master will reset the context. An example of this is shown in Figure 4-11.

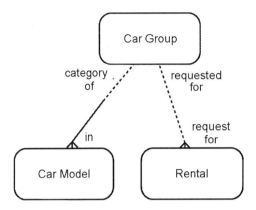

Figure 4-11 Example of logical discontinuity

In this example, it may be necessary to find out a specific Car Model that was allocated to the rental. If the navigation is from Rental through Car Group to Car Model, it will not be possible to identify the specific model allocated to the rental. Once the navigation path is at Car Group, it can only look at all the Car Models that belong to the Car Group. To tie up a specific Rental with a specific Car Model, it is necessary to have an access path that either goes direct from Rental to Car Model or via a detail entity for which Rental and Car Model are both masters.

Another situation to be aware of is where there are two alternative access paths from one entity to another, each of which may locate a different entity occurrence of the target entity. An example of this is shown in Figure 4-12.

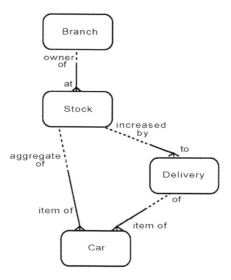

Figure 4-12 Example of circular relationships

In this example, to access Branch from Car, the access path via Stock gives the branch at which the car is currently located, whereas the access path via Delivery and Stock gives the branch to which the car was delivered when new.

4.4   Presenting the Logical Data Model to the user

It is important to get user acceptance of the accuracy of each Logical Data Model. They should be shown on a regular, informal basis to users (and the rest of the project team) as they are being developed to improve accuracy.

If users find it difficult to review the model as a diagram, consider reviewing the model using only the relationship statements. These can be a powerful way of testing the assumptions that have been made in building the model.

The ultimate test of the quality of the model is the demonstration that all required information support can be provided from a database based on the model

4.5   Logical Data Modelling and the Corporate Data Model

The guidance given in this volume and the assumes that the Logical Data Model is developed in isolation from other areas of the Organisation. However, it is possible that the Organisation surrounding the project will impose some constraints on the project in order that the Logical Data Model produced conforms to organisational standards.

One area of standardisation that will affect the Logical Data Modelling on a project is where the Organisation has developed a Corporate Data Model.

Corporate Data Models have been employed as part of the process of information systems development in a wide variety of situations and with varied success. A Corporate Data Model comprises a set of definitions for things of significance to the Organisation about which information needs to be held. In this, it is like any other model of business entities. What distinguishes a 'Corporate' model from any other is its scope, which extends across a number of applications systems.

The main function of such a model is to harmonise the definitions of data that are shared between different sub-systems. The model has to capture information about data interchange between sub-systems and identify data that passes between different areas.

A Corporate Data Model should help individual projects developing sub- systems by identifying the interfaces with which they must operate. The concept of entity aspects should help in co-ordinating definitions of entities in the Corporate Data Model and individual project models.

A Corporate Data Model may constrain the way in which the Logical Data Model for a particular project is developed. The Corporate Data Modelling infrastructure is likely to contain standards for the way in which data is modelled, naming of entities and attributes and the identification of entities and relationships. In addition a Corporate Data Model may provide grouped domains which constrain the definition of data items and therefore attributes.

If project is required to be undertaken in an Organisation where Corporate Data Modelling has been adopted, this must be taken into account when planning the approach to Logical Data Modelling. Where definitions of entities and attributes already exist within the Corporate Data Model, these should be adopted on the project. Data naming standards will need to be understood and used within the project. From time to time on the project, co-ordination points will need to be identified where the project Logical Data Model is compared to the Corporate Data Model and any discrepancies resolved.

As a word of caution, however, adherence to a Corporate Data Model may work in opposition to the validation of the Logical Data Model against functional requirements. A Corporate Data Model can only be constructed by examining the data and its perceived structure. A project Logical Data Model should be constructed to satisfy the requirements of the users for information support to the area of the business under investigation. Conflicts between project Logical Data Models and a Corporate Data Model may need to be carefully considered and resolved.

4.6   Fourth and Fifth Normal Form

In addition to the three steps of Third Normal Form it is possible to have two extra steps. These are Fourth and Fifth Normal Form. These are not normally used for most projects as Third Normal Form is felt to be adequate. These are described below and if thought useful they could be used on sources which require a very detailed analysis (e.g. where a whole system revolves around one crucial form).

4.6.1 Fourth normal form

Fourth Normal Form supports a special case of derived data in which a many-to-many relationship is maintained via a common master of two entities, rather than a jointly-owned detail.

For example an extension of EU-Rent is proposed, in which EU-Rent has different customer benefit programmes in different countries, and where customers might be registered in more than one country.

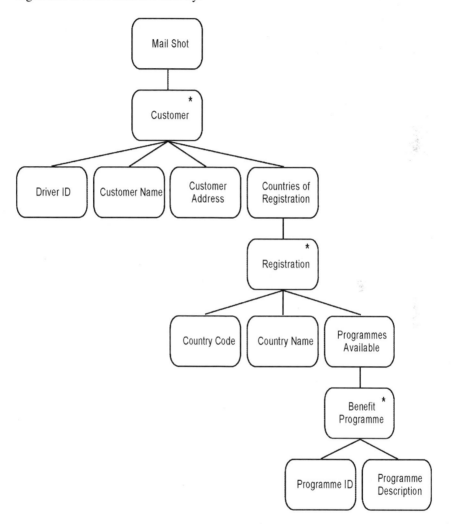

Figure 4-13 Mail shot output structure

Suppose that one of the required outputs was a mail shot, which informed each customer which benefit programmes he or she might join. The output structure is shown in Figure 4-13.

The results of Third Normal Form Analysis are shown in Figure 4-14.

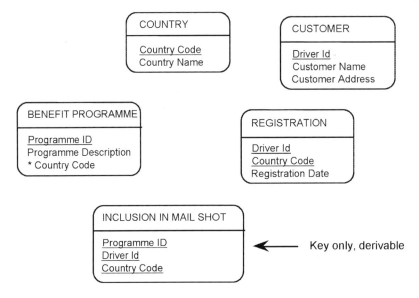

Figure 4-14: 3rd Normal Form of Mail Shot

The relation 'Inclusion in Mail Shot' can be derived. Each customer is to be informed of every programme available in each country in which he is registered. The system will maintain relations with Country Code as part of the key structure:

- Benefit Programme   (primary key: Programme ID, foreign key: Country Code)
- Registration   (primary key: Country Code / Driver ID)

Then, for a given value of Country Code, every value of Programme ID that appears in rows of Benefit Programme can be combined with every value of Driver ID that appears in rows of Registration, to create rows of Inclusion in Mail Shot. Thus Inclusion in Mail Shot is derivable and can be discarded.

(Note that in some systems there are requirements to keep a history of some types of output, and to be able to recreate them even if there have been subsequent changes to entities used in them. This is not the case in EU-Rent. If it were, the relation keys would be more complex than in the example.)

In logical data structuring terms, what has happened is that there is a many-to-many relationship between Benefit Programme and Registration, but it is maintained via the joint master, Country, rather than requiring a common detail.

At Third Normal Form, any relation with more than two keys and no data should be examined. If it can be decomposed into smaller relations such that the original relation can be reconstructed by combining valid values of the keys of the smaller relations, then it is a Fourth Normal Form derivable relation and can be discarded.

If there is any data dependent on the key, the relation cannot be derived. But sometimes, Fourth Normal Form structures are needed for construction of outputs, in addition to a non-derivable relation with the same key.

When the example was used earlier, there was a relation, Programme Membership, that had the same key as Inclusion in Mail Shot.

```
┌─────────────────────────────────────┐
│  PROGRAMME MEMBERSHIP                │
│                                      │
│  Programme ID                        │
│  Driver Id                           │
│  Country Code                        │
│  Programme Joining Date              │
└─────────────────────────────────────┘
```

Figure 4-15 3NF relation with same key as 4NF relation

It is important to recognise that the Fourth Normal Form relation is what is needed for the mail shot. If not, problems might occur. For example:

- the 3-part key will appear in the analysis of the Mail Shot output structure

- it could be mechanically matched (e.g. by a CASE tool) with the key of Programme Membership

- Programme Membership could then be cross-referenced with Mail Shot as the entity required for mail shot inclusion

The result would not be what was intended – the mail shot would go to customers who are already members of benefit schemes, rather than those whom EU-Rent hopes to attract.

4.6.2 Fifth normal form

A Fifth Normal Form structure is a Fourth Normal Form structure in which some of the rows of the derivable relation are excluded.

For example, suppose that EU-Rent wanted the mail shot to exclude mention of benefit programmes to which customers already belonged. The derivable relation Inclusion in Mail Shot would then be:

All combinations of Country Code, Driver ID and Programme ID that can be created by combining, for each Country Code, all the Driver IDs (in Registration) and all the Programme IDs (in Benefit Scheme), but excluding any row whose key appears in a row of Programme Membership.

In the example, the constraining relation, Programme Membership, has attributes. This does not have to be the case. There might have been, for example, a key-only relation representing customer preferences - i.e. that customers have indicated in the past that there are some programmes they are not interested in, and do not wish to hear about.

Note that the kind of 'table matching' implied by Fifth Normal Form ('the set of programmes to be included in a customer's mail shot letter is the difference between the set of all programmes for every country he is registered in, and the set of programmes for which he already has a membership') is not usually well-handled by application generators.

5 THE META MODEL FOR DATA MODELLING

The purpose of the concepts meta-model is to explain the concepts of the method in order to establish a common understanding between all parties interested in using and interpreting the method. This model attempts to identify the key concepts of the method and shows the interrelationships between the concepts. It should help to explain the products of Data Modelling in terms of their underlying interrelationships.[4]

The meta-model diagram is shown in Figure 5-1. Some points to note about the model in Figure 5-1areas follows:

- it is assumed that all elements of data within the system will be defined centrally as 'data items'. Each data item can then be used in a number of contexts, each one of which will be constrained by the definition of the data item. Attributes of entities are defined as data items in this way. The product which describes all data items centrally is the Data Catalogue described in the Logical Data Modelling chapter;

- all data items are defined by domains. A domain is a set of characteristics which are shared by a number of data items. It is assumed that domains can be hierarchical but that a data item can belong to only one domain. The product which describes domains is the Domain Description which is part of the Data Catalogue;

- the concept "entity aspect' indicates that the appearance of an entity on a Logical Data Model is simply one view of a more generalised entity. Where 'entity' might be expected to appear within the model, it is replaced by 'entity aspect'. In addition, each 'entity' can be represented by more than one aspect within the same Logical Data Model. An aspect is a view of an entity which has parallel behaviour to all other aspects of the same entity - aspects are not mutually exclusive and should not be confused with sub-types. This concept has been introduced for those situations where systems need to co-ordinate several representations of the same real-world entity;

- it is assumed here that a relationship can only be constrained by one exclusion for clarity. This meta-model does not support overlapping exclusions which may be required in more complex situations;

- it is assumed that each attribute 'belongs' to only one entity even though it may appear as part of the key structure for other entities.

---

[4] It should be stressed that this meta-model is not intended to be taken as a Logical Data Model and should not be considered as a database design for a repository. This is not a model of products and it does not attempt to show any transformations of one product into another or part-finished products in which the concepts are incomplete.

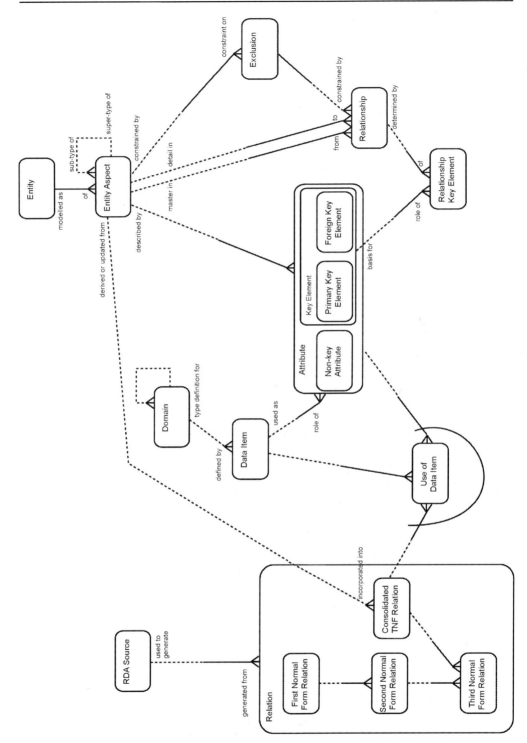

Figure 5-1 Meta-model of concepts

Descriptions for each of the major concepts are given in the table below:

Entity	Description
Attribute	A characteristic property of an entity type, that is, any detail that serves to describe, qualify, identify, classify, quantify or express the state of an entity aspect. Each attribute is defined as belonging to only one entity aspect. Identifying attributes may appear in more than one entity description to support relationships. Each attribute is described by a data item which is the general definition of any element of data, wherever it is used.
Data Item	Any element of data that is used within the system. Each data item may fulfil a number of different roles, each of which will be constrained by this central definition.
Domain	A set of characteristics shared by one or more Data Item.
Entity	Something, whether concrete or abstract, which is of relevance to the system and about which information needs to be stored. This concept represents a general definition of the entity that can be shared by a number of different systems/areas. It is an aspect of the entity that is represented within a specific project's Logical Data Model.
Entity Aspect	A view of an entity that is relevant to the system under investigation. There may be more than one aspect of the same entity represented on a single project's Logical Data Model. In most systems, only one aspect will need to be modelled so entity and aspect names are interchangeable.
Exclusion	A constraint on two or more relationships from the same entity aspect indicating that only one of the relationships can exist for each occurrence of the entity aspect.
Key Element	A type of attribute that is used as part of the primary key of one or more entity aspects or as a foreign key representing a relationship. These are the only types of attribute that can be included in more than one entity aspect.
Non-key attribute	A type of attribute which describes a characteristic of an entity but does not form part of the key structure. This type of attribute will belong to only one Entity Aspect.
RDA Source	The source as the input to Relational Data Analysis.
Relation	A relation is equivalent to an entity. It is defined as being a two-dimensional table; that is, it comprises a number of rows and a number of columns. Each column represents an attribute of the relation and each row represents the values that can be taken by each attribute.

Entity	Description
Relationship	An association between two entity aspects (or an entity aspect and itself) to which all instances of the relationship must conform.
Relationship Key Element	The inclusion of a specific key element attribute in a specific relationship indicating the foreign key or cascading primary key structure within the Logical Data Model. (The key element attribute and the relationship connected using this concept must belong to the same entity aspect.)

6   PRODUCT DESCRIPTIONS FOR DATA MODELLING

Listed below are the Product Descriptions for those products produced during Data
Modelling. These Product Descriptions should not be regarded as definitive, rather they are
a start point that can be tailored for each individual project. It is expected that each project
will examine the composition list and add and remove as necessary to suit their particular
project. In addition if a Case Tool is utilised then the Case Tool may have a suggested list
of its own.

6.1   Attribute/Data Item Descriptions

Purpose

To package all Attributes/Data Item Descriptions together.

Each description documents all of the details relating to a particular attribute or data item,
regardless of which technique has been used in obtaining the information. Only one central
description of an attribute or data item is to be maintained and accessed whenever
necessary.

In the logical system, 'attributes' are documented (though these may be thought of as
'logical data items'); these generally translate, during Database Design, into 'physical data
items' for the implemented system.

Composition

Each Attribute/Data Item Description entry consists of:

- Attribute/data item name.

- Attribute/data item identifier.

- Cross-reference details - repeating group consisting of:

    - cross-reference name/identifier;

    - cross-reference type.

- Synonyms.

- Description.

- Validation/derivation details.

- Default value.

- Logical details;

    - logical format

- logical length;
- length description.
- User Roles details – repeating group of:
    - user role name;
    - access rights.
- Owner.
- Standard messages.

Position in System Development Template

- Investigation.
- Specification – Conceptual Model.

Quality Criteria:

For each:

1 Has this been identified as an attribute or a data item?

2 Is the attribute assigned to one and only one entity?

3 Are the descriptions of entity and data item user role owners consistent?

4 Is the documentation complete (except where this details a state indicator)?

For the set:

5 Is the set complete?

6 Is the version number consistent throughout the set?

7 Is the set consistent with the previous version?

External Dependencies

None identified

6.2   Entity Descriptions

Purpose

To provide comprehensive documentation for all entities.

Each entity is fully described and packaged as part of the Logical Data Model.

Composition

Each Entity Description consists of the following:

Heading

- Entity:
    - Entity name;
    - Entity identifier;
    - Aspect/Sub-type/Super-type name.
- Number of occurrences:
    - average;
    - maximum.
- Description.
- Synonym(s).
- Attribute details, repeating group of:
    - attribute name/identifier;
    - mandatory/optional indicator;
    - mutually exclusive cross-reference to other attributes/data items;
    - primary key/foreign key.
- Relationship statements.
- User Role Details, repeating group of:
    - User role name;
    - access rights.
- Owner.
- Growth per period.
- Archive and destruction details.

- Security measures.
- State indicator values.

Position in System Development Template

Investigation.

Specification – Conceptual Model.

Quality Criteria:

For each Entity Description:

1   Is the variant identifier completed and valid?

2   Is this entity really an entity, i.e. a thing of significance about which information needs to be held?

3   Is the entity name singular and meaningful?

4   Does the entity have a primary key?

5   Is this entity fully defined?

6   Can you visualise instances of this entity?

7   Has volumetric information been included? (where known)

8   Are all attribute names singular and meaningful?

9   Have all attributes been identified for this entity?

10   Are the user role, access, and owner details consistent on the entity and attribute descriptions?

11   Have all entity synonyms been identified?

12   Are all fields complete?

13   Are relationships correctly represented as foreign keys?

For the set:

14   Is the set of entity descriptions complete for this version?

External Dependencies

None

6.3   Domain Description

Purpose

To document the details of a domain.

The concept of a domain is used informally in Logical Data Modelling to represent validation and formatting rules, permitted classes and ranges of values which are common to more than one attribute. For example, all 'Date' attributes would be based on the same domain, 'Dates'. A Domain Description may be used to record common attribute descriptions if this saves effort.

Composition

- Domain identification:
    - Domain name;
    - Domain identifier;
    - Cross-references;
    - Synonym(s);
    - Description;
    - Validation/Derivation;
    - Default value.
- Logical details:
    - Logical format;
    - Logical length;
    - Length description.
- User role details, repeating group of:
    - User role;
    - Access rights.
- Owner.
- Standard Messages.

Position in System Development Template

- Investigation.
- Specification – Conceptual Model

Quality Criteria:

1   Does the Domain Description apply to all the corresponding data items?

2   Where formatting and validation rules are further refined in individual Attribute/Data Item Descriptions, are these refinements consistent with the general rules in the Domain Description?

3   Does the domain include more than one attribute?

4   Is the information complete for this domain?

External Dependencies

None identified.

6.4   Logical Data Model (LDM)

Purpose

To provide a detailed logical description of the data and its structure.

Suitability

Current Environment

A Logical Data Model of the current environment is suitable where the information in the current situation is structured and definable, and where much of the structure will provide the basis of the design of the future system. It is also suitable where the scope of the investigation is clearly defined, and where it is necessary to understand the existing data requirements and to inform future requirements definition. When there is no current system, the system requirements should be interpreted into an initial LDM for clarity.

A Logical Data Model is suitable where the:

- complexity of information is high;
- stability of the environment is high;
- formality of current information is high;
- understanding of existing system is high;
- quality of existing specifications is high;
- stability of information is high.

Required System

The Logical Data Model is an essential element of a IS/IT project and is one of the underlying principles on which the computer system is built. It may be partitioned into sub-systems for phased development or evolutionary growth. It is suitable where any sort of database is required, particularly where the detailed behaviour of the data is to be studied.

A Logical Data Model is suitable where the:

- complexity of data is high;
- formality of information is high;
- specificity and stability of data is high;
- flexibility and portability of the proposed system is an objective.

Composition

This is a composite product consisting of:

- Logical Data Structure (LDS);
- Entity Descriptions;
- Relationship Descriptions.

Notes:

Logical Data Modelling also generates information about attributes. The Attribute/Data Item Descriptions and Domain Descriptions are maintained within the Data Catalogue.

Position in System Development Template

- Investigation.
- Specification – Conceptual Model

Quality Criteria:

1   Is the model variant (e.g. current environment or required system) correctly and consistently assigned to all components of the model?

2   Is every entity depicted in the Logical Data Structure also described in the Entity Descriptions?

3   Is every relationship depicted in the Logical Data Structure also described in the Relationship Descriptions?

4   Are only entities depicted in the Logical Data Structure also described in the Entity Descriptions?

5   Are only relationships depicted in the Logical Data Structure also described in the Relationship Descriptions?

6   Is the model consistent with previous versions?

External Dependencies

Availability of users for discussions to develop the Current Environment Logical Data Model.

6.5   Logical Data Structure (LDS)

Purpose

To provide a logical structure of the non-transient system data.

Composition

A graphical representation using entity-relationship modelling. See the Logical Data Modelling chapter for more detail.

Position in System Development Template

- Investigation.
- Specification – Conceptual Model.

Quality Criteria:

1	Is the variant identifier completed correctly?
2	Is each entity really an entity, i.e., a thing of significance about which information needs to be held? (Can you imagine instances?)
3	Are all entity names singular and meaningful?
4	Does each entity have a unique identifier?
5	Is each relationship really a relationship, i.e. a significant association between entities?
6	Is each relationship end named and capable of being read accurately and sensibly?
7	Does each relationship begin at an entity and end at an entity?
8	Do all relationship ends in an exclusive arc have the same optionality?
9	Is the structure consistent with the previous version of the LDS?
10	Have all m:n relationships been resolved (Required System only)?
11	If mandatory relationships, will there always be an occurrence of the entity at the other end?

12   Are any relationships redundant?

13   Are all the entities in Third Normal Form (Required System only)?

Quality Method:

Apply Third Normal Form tests:

- Given a value for the key(s) of a Third Normal Form relation, is there only one possible value for each of the associated data items? If the answer is 'NO' the relation is not in Third Normal Form.

- Is each data item directly dependent on the key(s)? If the answer is 'NO' the relation is not in Third Normal Form.

External Dependencies

- Overview LDS: note that if a Feasibility Study has been carried out this product may not be required.

- Availability of users for discussions to develop the Current Environment LDM.

6.6   RDA (Relational Data Analysis) Working Paper

Purpose

To validate the Logical Data Model, which will have been developed top-down, against relations developed bottom-up.

Composition

Heading:

- Source Name.

Entries consisting of:

- un-normalised form;
- attribute;
- level;
- First Normal Form (1NF);
- Second Normal Form (2NF);
- Third Normal Form (3NF) Result:
    - relation;
    - attributes.

Position in System Development Template

- Specification - Conceptual Model

Quality Criteria:

1   Are the normalisation rules applied correctly at each stage?

2   Are any candidate (non-primary) keys redundant?

External Dependencies

None.

6.7   Relationship Descriptions

Purpose

To provide detailed documentation for all relationships on the Logical Data Structure. There will be two elements of documentation completed for every relationship on the Logical Data Structure.

A full set of the documentation is packaged within the Logical Data Model.

Composition

Heading:

- Logical Data Model variant identifier, one of:
    - Current Environment;
    - Required System.
- Entities;
- Entity names;
- Entity identifiers.

Relationship Description:

- Mandatory/optional indicator.
- Percentage optional.
- Link phrase.
- Description.
- Synonym(s).
- Number of occurrences: minimum, maximum, average.
- Cardinality description.
- Growth per period.
- Additional properties.
- Owner.

Position in System Development Template

- Investigation
- Specification – Conceptual Model

Quality Criteria:

For each:

1   Is the variant identifier completed correctly?

2   Is this relationship really a relationship, i.e. a significant association between entities?

3   Is each relationship end named and capable of being read accurately and sensibly?

4   Does each relationship end have the correct degree and optionality?

5   If mandatory relationships, will there always be an occurrence of the entity at the other end?

6   Is all mandatory information complete?

7   Has retention of historical data been catered for correctly?

For the set:

8   Is the set of Relationship Descriptions complete?

External Dependencies

None

ANNEXE A – DESCRIPTION OF SYSTEM DEVELOPMENT TEMPLATE

The System Development Template (SDT) provides a common structure for the overall system development process. This template is used extensively in the definition of SSADM.

The System Development Template divides the development process into a number of distinct areas of concern, as shown in the diagram below.

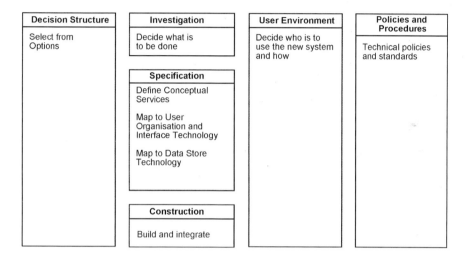

Figure A-1 System Development Template general view

The 3-schema specification architecture (which covers the Specification area) concentrates on those products that will ultimately lead, sometimes via other products, into elements of software. The SDT takes a broader view and divides the system development process into activity areas onto which all the development products may be mapped.

ANNEXE B – DESCRIPTION OF EU-RENT CASE STUDY

EU-Rent is a car rental company owned by EU-Corporation. It is one of three businesses – the other two being hotels and an airline – that each have their own business and IT systems, but share their customer base. Many of the car rental customers also fly with EU-Fly and stay at EU-Stay hotels.

EU-Rent business

EU-Rent has 1000 branches in towns all over Europe. At each branch cars, classified by car group, are available for rental. Each branch has a manager and booking clerks who handle rentals.

Rentals

Most rentals are by advance reservation; the rental period and the car group are specified at the time of reservation. EU-Rent will also accept immediate ('walk-in') rentals, if cars are available.

At the end of each day cars are assigned to reservations for the following day. If more cars have been requested than are available in a group at a branch, the branch manager may ask other branches if they have cars they can transfer to him/her.

Returns

Cars rented from one branch of EU-Rent may be returned to any other branch. The renting branch must ensure that the car has been returned to some branch at the end of the rental period. If a car is returned to a branch other than the one that rented it, ownership of the car is assigned to the new branch.

Servicing

EU-Rent also has service depots, each serving several branches. Cars may be booked for maintenance at any time provided that the service depot has capacity on the day in question.

For simplicity, only one booking per car per day is allowed. A rental or service may cover several days.

Customers

A customer can have several reservations but only one car rented at a time. EU-Rent keeps records of customers, their rentals and bad experiences such as late return, problems with payment and damage to cars. This information is used to decide whether to approve a rental.

Current IT system

Each branch and service depot has a local IT system based on PCs and a file server. The equipment is obsolete and limited in capacity (especially RAM). Hardware failures – screens, disk drives and power supplies – are increasingly frequent. There is currently no use of the Internet either for customer to business communication or for business to business communication.

Application maintainability

The application programs have been maintained over several years. Small RAM in the PCs has necessitated intricate, complex programs which makes amendments progressively more difficult and expensive.

Informal communication

Each location operates almost independently of others. Communication between locations is mainly by phone and fax and co-ordination is very variable. Sometimes, when a car is dropped off at a branch different from the pick-up branch, the drop-off branch will not inform the pick-up branch.

Branch managers tend to co-operate in small groups and not to look for 'spare' cars outside those groups. EU-Rent management feels that some capacity is wasted, but does not have reliable estimates of how much.

Scheduling of service bookings in branch and service depot files is co-ordinated by faxes between branch and depot. Sometimes service bookings are not recorded in the branch files, and cars booked for servicing are rented. Service depots sometimes do not get to know that a car has been transferred to a branch served by other depots until another depot requests the car's service history.

Customer blacklist

A copy of the customer blacklist is held at every branch. It should be updated every week from head office, but the logistics of updating the list with input from 1000 sources and sending out 1000 disks every week are beyond head office's capability. Updates are in fact sent out about every four weeks.

E-Commerce

There is no current use of e-commerce with customers having to phone or fax the individual offices to book cars for rental. This is causing problems in that some competitors have introduced facilities that enable customers to book and monitor their bookings over the Internet and it is thought that this is resulting in a loss of custom.

IT system replacement

EU-Rent management has decided that a new IT system is needed. It is expected whilst the basic operational activity is not expected to change significantly – locations and volume of rentals – it is expected that a number of 'online' systems (e.g. ordering of cars) will be implemented not necessarily as part of the initial role out but shortly thereafter. The new system is justified on three grounds:

- the current system cannot be kept going much longer;

- the perceived need to introduce some online system that can be accessed directly by customers over the Internet;

- better management of numbers of cars at branches and better co-ordination between branches is expected to increase utilisation of cars slightly – the same volume of business should be supportable with fewer cars. Each car ties up about 8,000 Euros in capital and loses about 3,000 Euros in depreciation, so significant savings are possible from small reductions in numbers of cars needed.

Corporate data

After the current IT system has been replaced, EU-Rent management wants to explore possibilities for sharing customer data across the car rental, hotel and airline systems. Even if customers are not stored in a single shared database, it makes sense for all three business areas to have consistent customer information on current address, telephone number, credit rating, etc.

It will be useful to know in each system when there are problems with a customer in other systems. And it may be possible to run promotions in one system, based on what EU-Corporation knows from the other systems about customers.

Future requirements

A customer loyalty incentive scheme is also under consideration. The requirement is not yet precisely defined but the scheme will be comparable with those offered by EU-Rent's competitors.

Members of the scheme will accumulate credit points with each car rental. They will exchange points for 'free' rentals. Only the base rental price will be payable by points; extra charges such as insurance and fuel will be paid for by cash or credit card. When this is introduced it is expected that customers will wish to be able to check (either by the use of a call-centre or directly over the Internet) the current state of their credit points.

Rationale for EU-Rent

The business of EU-Rent is car rentals, but this is largely irrelevant; it merely provides an easily understood context for examples. The business issues and user requirements in EU-Rent could be easily mapped to other systems. They include:

- a requirement to deliver a range of services (rental of cars of different quality and price) at many locations (rental branches), with different volumes of business and patterns of demand;

- customers who may use more than one location, but whose business with the whole organisation should be tracked;

- strong general policies set centrally (car models that may be used, rental tariffs, procedures for dealing with customers), but significant flexibility and authority for local managers (number of cars owned by branch, authority to over-ride published tariff to beat competitors' prices);

- a requirement for customers to be able to directly access aspects of the system;

- performance targets for local managers;

- a requirement for capacity planning and resource replenishment (disposal and purchase of cars, moving of cars between branches); possibilities for this to be managed locally, regionally or centrally;

- locally-managed sharing or swapping of resources or customers between branches to meet short-term unforeseen demand;

- an internal support structure (the maintenance depots) needed to maintain the resources and ensure that the product delivered to customers is of adequate quality;

- a customer base that is shared with other, separate systems (EU-Stay hotels and EU-Fly airline), and possibilities of communicating or co-ordinating with these systems.

Many of these characteristics are common to other types of business; for example, health care, vocational training, social security, policing, retail chain stores, branch banking.

ANNEXE C – GLOSSARY OF TERMS

attribute

A characteristic property of an entity, or entity aspect, that is, any detail that serves to describe, qualify, identify, classify, quantify or express the state of an entity.

An attribute may be optional for an entity, meaning that it does not always have a value for all occurrences of the entity.

Attributes can form part of the primary key of the entity or may appear as foreign keys. Non-key attributes may belong to only one entity/entity aspect after normalisation.

Each attribute is described by a data item which is the general definition of any element of data, wherever it is used.

Attribute/Data Item Description

Each description documents all known details about a data item. These details are true for the data item wherever it is referenced. Details can include length, format, validation details and derivation.

candidate key

A candidate key is any (minimal) set of one or more attributes that can for all time be used as a unique identifier of an entity or relation. 'Minimal' means that no subset of those attributes identified as a candidate key is also a candidate key.

For each relation or entity, one candidate key must be selected as the primary key which is used consistently throughout the system.

CASE tools

Computer-aided Software Engineering (CASE) tools are automated tools supporting analysts in their use of development techniques. This type of tool normally supports the diagrammatic techniques as well as containing a repository of information supporting the diagrams.

Conceptual Model

System Development Template component

The Conceptual Model comprises the essential business rules and knowledge. It is a system model which is independent of the user interface and hence is portable between different implementation environments. It is possible to believe, in some respects, that there is a 'right' answer to Conceptual Model design. Most projects express the Conceptual Model as a Logical Data Model and models of the interaction between entities and events/enquiries .

Current Environment Logical Data Model

Provides a detailed description of the information used or produced by the current environment. See also entries and Product Description for Logical Data Model.

Data Catalogue

The central repository for all the descriptive information about items of data. In addition to logical details this can include physical details. Logical data modelling will provide information about attributes (the logical equivalent to data items).

Data Item/Attribute Description

Synonym for Attribute/Data Item Description.

data store

A collection of any type of data in any form as represented on a Data Flow Diagram. In the Current Physical Data Flow Model, this may be a computer file or a box of documents or any other means of storing data. These are cross-referenced against entities on the Logical Data Model

entity

Something, whether concrete or abstract, which is of relevance to the system and about which information needs to be stored. This concept represents a general definition of the entity that can be shared by a number of different systems/ areas. It is the aspect of the entity relevant to the system under investigation that is represented within a specific project's Logical Data Model.

entity aspect

A view of an entity that is relevant to the system under investigation. There may be more than one aspect of the same entity represented on a single project's Logical Data Model. In most systems, only one aspect will need to be modelled so entity and aspect names are interchangeable.

Entity Description

Documents all of the details concerned with entities on the Logical Data Structure.

exclusion

A constraint on two or more relationships from the same entity (or entity aspect) on a Logical Data Structure indicating that only one of the relationships can exist for each occurrence of the entity (or entity aspect).

exclusive relationship group

If the participation of an entity occurrence in one relationship precludes its participation in one or more other relationships this identifies an 'exclusive relationship group'.

External Design

System Development Template element

The External Design comprises the user interface: data definitions for input/output files, screens and reports; process definitions for dialogue input/output programs. External Design depends on trade-offs between many factors, for example, ergonomics, system efficiency and users' various subjective preferences. This is a creative area and heuristic approaches, such as prototyping, can have a role here. The External Design passes event data and enquiry triggers to the Conceptual Model, and receives event and enquiry output in response.

First Normal Form (1NF)

see entry for Normal Form

foreign key

A foreign key is defined as a non-key attribute (or group of related non-key attributes) in one relation or entity which is the same as the key of another relation or entity.

.

Internal Design

System Development Template element

The Internal Design defines the physical database design and the process/data interface. There is a dependency on trade-offs, between such factors as timing, space utilisation and maintainability. It is a creative area where there is no 'right' answer. Heuristic approaches may be appropriate.

Investigation

System Development Template element

Includes decisions on what is to be done based upon investigation of what is currently done, Business Activity Modelling and Requirements Definition.

Logical Data Model

Provides an accurate model of the information requirements of all or part of an organisation. This serves as a basis for file and database design, but is independent of any specific implementation technique or product.

The Logical Data Model consists of a Logical Data Structure, Entity Descriptions and Relationship Descriptions. Associated descriptions of attribute/data items and domains are maintained in the Data Catalogue.

Logical Data Modelling

Logical Data Modelling is used to investigate and model the structured data that is held within a system as information support to business activities. The technique is used to both model the data of the current system and to build a model of what are the data requirements of the new system.

Logical Data Modelling is at the very heart of nearly all projects.

Logical Data Structure

A diagrammatic representation of the information needs of an organisation in the form of entities and the relationships between them.

The Logical Data Structure formalises the structure of information by depicting diagrammatically the different types of relationship in which entities can participate.

A Logical Data Structure consists of two basic components:

- entities;
- relationships.

master entity

Where two entities are connected by a 1:m relationship, a single occurrence of one entity is related to several occurrences of the other. The entity at the 'single' end is deemed the master entity.

See also detail entity.

Normal Form

Is the result of applying the Relational Data Analysis technique to groupings of data input to or output from the system. There are several stages of normalisation; relations are translated into:

- First Normal Form (1NF)

- Second Normal Form (2NF)

- Third Normal Form (3NF)

primary key

A primary key is an attribute or a combination of attributes which can be used to uniquely identify an entity or relation.

quality criteria

Characteristics of a product which determine whether it meets requirements, and thus define what 'quality' means in the context of that product. These are defined in the Product Descriptions and agreed with the project board before development of the product commences.

RDA Working Paper

Is used to document the progress through relational data analysis, taking relations which are un-normalised through to third normal form.

relation

A relation is a group of data items (or attributes). When the Logical Data Model is validated using relational data analysis, a relation equates to an entity.

Relational Data Analysis

Is a method of deriving data structures which have the least redundant data and the most flexibility. The flexibility is achieved by breaking down the data groups into smaller groups without losing any of the original information. It is the objective of this technique to transform all relations into at least third normal form.

'Normalisation' uses rules to analyse the way items of data depend upon one another for their meaning.

In a 'normalised Logical Data Model' all entities, considered as relations, must be in third (or higher) normal form.

relationship

Is an association between two entities (entity aspects), or one entity (aspect) and itself (recursion/involution), to which all instances (occurrences) of the relationship must conform.

Relationship Description

Documents the details of a relationship between two entities on the Logical Data Structure. Part of the Logical Data Model.

Required System Logical Data Model

Provides the detail of the proposed system information requirements. It is developed during the Requirements Specification and Logical System Specification Modules. It is compared with the results of Relational Data Analysis to produce a normalised model.

See also Logical Data Model.

Second Normal Form (2NF)

see entry for Normal Form.

sub-type

An entity representing a particular alternative behaviour of the corresponding super-type entity. A sub-type contains all the attributes which are specific to that sub-type only. Sub-types of the same super-type are always alternatives of each other.

super-type

An entity which has several different alternative behaviours such that each occurrence of the entity is of a particular type.

System Development Template

The System Development Template provides a common structure for the overall system development process.

- It divides the process into a number of distinct areas of concern:
- Investigation;
- Specification;
- Construction;
- Decision Structure;
- User Organisation;
- Policies and Procedures.

The Specification area contains a further breakdown which is made up of the areas Conceptual Model, Internal design and External Design.

Third Normal Form (3NF)

see entry for Normal Form.

INDEX